DANIEL

Text copyright © Doug Ingram 2006

The author asserts the moral right to be
identified as the author of this work

Published by
The Bible Reading Fellowship
First Floor, Elsfield Hall
15–17 Elsfield Hall, Oxford OX2 8FG
Website: www.brf.org.uk

ISBN-10: 1 84101 395 1
ISBN-13: 978 1 84101 395 4

First published 2006
10 9 8 7 6 5 4 3 2 1 0

Acknowledgments
Scripture quotations taken from The New Revised Standard Version of
the Bible, Anglicized Edition, copyright © 1989, 1995 by the Division of
Christian Education of the National Council of the Churches of Christ in
the United States of America, are used by permission. All rights reserved.

Scripture quotations taken from the *Holy Bible, New International Version*,
copyright © 1973, 1978, 1984 by International Bible Society. Used by
permission of Hodder & Stoughton Ltd. All rights reserved. 'NIV' is a
registered trademark of International Bible Society. UK trademark
number 1448790.

New King James Version of the Bible copyright © 1979, 1980, 1982 by
Thomas Nelson, Inc. All rights reserved.

A catalogue record for this book is available from the British Library

Printed in Singapore by Craft Print International Ltd

DANIEL

THE PEOPLE'S
BIBLE COMMENTARY

DOUG
INGRAM

A BIBLE COMMENTARY FOR EVERY DAY

INTRODUCING THE
PEOPLE'S BIBLE COMMENTARY
SERIES

Congratulations! You are embarking on a voyage of discovery—or rediscovery. You may feel you know the Bible very well; you may never have turned its pages before. You may be looking for a fresh way of approaching daily Bible study; you may be searching for useful insights to share in a study group or from a pulpit.

The People's Bible Commentary (PBC) series is designed for all those who want to study the scriptures in a way that will warm the heart as well as instructing the mind. To help you, the series distils the best of scholarly insights into the straightforward language and devotional emphasis of Bible reading notes. Explanation of background material, and discussion of the original Greek and Hebrew, will always aim to be brief.

* If you have never really studied the Bible before, the series offers a serious yet accessible way in.

* If you help to lead a church study group, or are otherwise involved in regular preaching and teaching, you can find invaluable 'snapshots' of a Bible passage through the PBC approach.

* If you are a church worker or minister, burned out on the Bible, this series could help you recover the wonder of scripture.

Using a People's Bible Commentary

The series is designed for use alongside any version of the Bible. You may have your own favourite translation, but you might like to consider trying a different one in order to gain fresh perspectives on familiar passages.

Many Bible translations come in a range of editions, including study and reference editions that have concordances, various kinds of special index, maps and marginal notes. These can all prove helpful in studying the relevant passage. The Notes section at the back of each PBC volume provides space for you to write personal reflections, points to follow up, questions and comments.

Each People's Bible Commentary can be used on a daily basis, instead of Bible reading notes. Alternatively, it can be read straight through, or used as a resource book for insight into particular verses of the biblical book.

If you have enjoyed using this commentary and would like to progress further in Bible study, you will find details of other volumes in the series listed at the back, together with information about a special offer from BRF.

While it is important to deepen understanding of a given passage, this series always aims to engage both heart and mind in the study of the Bible. The scriptures point to our Lord himself and our task is to use them to build our relationship with him. When we read, let us do so prayerfully, slowly, reverently, expecting him to speak to our hearts.

CONTENTS

PBC DANIEL: INTRODUCTION

Daniel is a fascinating and enigmatic book. Some of the stories in the first half of the book are very well known, both by people who use the Bible regularly and by others who have little to do with church—especially the story of Daniel in the lions' den, and to a lesser extent the story of Shadrach, Meshach and Abednego in the fiery furnace. In terms of the history of interpretation of the book of Daniel, the images from the 'apocalyptic' visions in the second half of the book have attracted most attention, especially the 'one like a son of man' (NIV) in chapter 7, and to a lesser extent the 'abomination that desolates', which appears a number of times. The 'abomination that desolates' is picked up explicitly in the Gospels, and it seems very likely that Jesus draws on the 'one like a son of man' as part of the background to his self-designation as 'the Son of Man'. Moreover, the book of Daniel is a very important element in the key aspect of Jesus' teaching, the kingdom of God. Kingdom language (words like 'king', 'kingdom' or 'kingship', 'rule', sovereignty' and so on) appears more in Daniel than anywhere else in the Old Testament, and here, as in the Gospels, God's kingdom has a dual aspect: it is already established but will only be fully realized at some point in the future. The imagery from Daniel is also extensively drawn upon in the book of Revelation in the New Testament.

One scholar writes, 'Daniel is a very curious book in many respects. From almost every standpoint it presents a dual character: it contains two kinds of material, apparently intended originally for two different audiences; its contents relate to two different times and places; it has two canonical forms; and it is written in two languages' (Davies, p. 11). Most of the rest of this introduction will explore this 'dual character'.

Two kinds of material

The book of Daniel readily falls into two halves. The first six chapters consist of six stories relating events in Daniel's life (and in the lives of his three friends, Shadrach, Meshach and Abednego), while the final six chapters describe four very strange visions that Daniel had. The stories are delightful (although they include some darker elements), and, at least superficially, are easy to follow and understand. The visions are odd, contain some rather gruesome imagery and are decidedly allusive and difficult to pin down. The stories appear straightforward (and actually their main themes are obvious); the visions are anything but straightforward. The stories and visions may be outlined as follows.

Story 1:
Daniel and friends in the Babylonian court

In chapter 1, we learn that Daniel and three other Jewish young men (Hananiah, Mishael and Azariah, renamed Shadrach, Meshach and Abednego; Daniel was renamed Belteshazzar) were among the exiles taken by King Nebuchadnezzar from Judah to Babylon. In Babylon they were trained in Babylonian ways to serve in the king's palace, but they refused to eat the rich food and to drink the wine they were given, insisting instead that they eat only vegetables and drink only water. At the end of a trial period, they not only proved much healthier than those who had accepted the rich food and wine, but they also had greater understanding and wisdom than the Babylonian wise men. Such wisdom and understanding were, of course, given to them by God.

Story 2:
Daniel interprets Nebuchadnezzar's first dream

Chapter 2 describes how the Babylonian king, Nebuchadnezzar, had a strange dream of a great statue made of various materials, which was destroyed by a stone. Unable to interpret the vision, he called on all his wise men not only to interpret the dream, but even to tell him what the dream was. While they could not, Daniel both related the dream and told Nebuchadnezzar what it meant: the various materials from which the statue was constructed represented successive kingdoms of which Nebuchadnezzar's was the first; the stone represented the kingdom that God would set up, which would destroy all the other kingdoms but would never be destroyed itself. As a result of relating the dream and interpreting it for Nebuchadnezzar, Daniel was promoted to high office. Upon his request, Shadrach, Meshach and Abednego were also promoted.

Story 3:
The fiery furnace

Chapter 3 relates that Nebuchadnezzar had a huge golden statue built and insisted that everyone bow down to the statue when a selection of musical instruments sounded. Punishment for disobeying this command was to be thrown into a furnace. Shadrach, Meshach and Abednego refused to bow down and were therefore thrown into the furnace. Not only did they survive unharmed, but while they were there Nebuchadnezzar saw a fourth figure with them whom he understood to be an angel from God. Shadrach, Meshach and Abednego were released and promoted to even higher positions.

Story 4:
Daniel interprets Nebuchadnezzar's second dream

Again Nebuchadnezzar had a dream, described in chapter 4, which he couldn't understand. Again the Babylonian wise men couldn't interpret it for him, and again Daniel could. The dream this time was of a great tree which was chopped down, and it related to Nebuchadnezzar himself: he had become too proud and as a result God would take his kingdom away from him for seven years. The kingdom would be restored to him only when he humbled himself before God. The dream came true and Nebuchadnezzar praised Daniel's God because of it.

Story 5:
Daniel is used by God to humble Belshazzar

In chapter 5, we encounter a different king, Belshazzar, who is described as Nebuchadnezzar's son. He is pictured as an arrogant man who threw a huge party, using silver and gold vessels taken from the temple in Jerusalem for the food and drink. In the middle of his great party, a mysterious hand appeared and wrote something on the wall that neither Belshazzar nor any of his wise men could understand. Daniel was summoned. He explained that the words related God's judgment on Belshazzar and predicted his death that very night. Indeed, Belshazzar did die that night as the Babylonian kingdom fell to the Persians, but before he died he promoted Daniel to 'third in the kingdom'.

Story 6:
Daniel in the lion's den

The king in chapter 6 is the Persian king, Darius. At the suggestion of his leading officials, he issued a decree that no one must pray to anyone but him for 30 days, upon penalty of death. Daniel continued to pray to God three times a day, in front of a window open towards Jerusalem, and Darius' officials pointed this out to the king. Darius had no option but to have Daniel cast into a den of lions (the stipulated punishment), although he didn't want to do it. The following morning, Darius returned to the lions' den to discover that Daniel had survived. Darius had him taken out and the officials and their families thrown in instead. Darius then decreed that everyone should 'tremble and fear before the God of Daniel'.

Vision 1:
Daniel's alternating vision

Chapter 7 consists of a vision that Daniel saw, which alternates between two scenes. In one scene, four grotesque beasts arise from the sea one by one; the other seems to be set in heaven, where an 'ancient one' sits on his throne and 'one like a human being' appears before him. The explanation of this vision given to Daniel indicates that the four beasts represent successive human kingdoms, which are judged by the 'ancient one' for the way they act. Dominion is taken away from them and given instead to the 'one like a human being' and to 'the holy ones of the Most High'.

Vision 2:
Daniel's vision of a ram and a goat

Unlike the previous vision, the one of a ram and a goat in chapter 8 is explained in relation to specific human empires. The ram is the Medo-Persian empire that followed the Babylonian empire (of which Nebuchadnezzar was a king), and it is followed by the Greek empire, represented by a goat. The ram had two horns, representing the kings of Media and Persia. The goat had a great horn, which was broken, to be replaced by four horns. Out of one of these horns a little horn sprouted, which grew exceedingly great. It is this little horn that is the climax of the vision. Although the text doesn't identify the horn, it is generally agreed that it represents the second-century BC ruler Antiochus IV Epiphanes, who instigated terrible oppression of the Jews.

Vision 3:
Daniel's prayer and the vision of 70 weeks

Most of chapter 9 consists of a prayer that Daniel prays to God, in which he confesses the sins of his people and asks for God to act on their behalf and for God's own reputation. The chapter concludes with a further vision in which Daniel is told about 70 weeks that are decreed for his people. The 70 weeks are broken down into seven weeks, 62 weeks and one final week, which has two halves. The climax of these weeks is 'an abomination that desolates' in the first half of the last week, followed by the decreed end of the desolator.

Vision 4:
Daniel's vision of kings of the south and north

The final vision has an introduction in chapter 10 and a conclusion at the end of chapter 12. In between lies the vision proper, which tells of various kings of the north and kings of the south. It builds up to the final king of the north, who wreaks havoc upon Jerusalem and the temple and sets up 'the abomination that makes desolate'. The death of this king is related at the end of chapter 11, before chapter 12 describes what will happen to 'the holy ones' following this king's death (or at 'the time of the end'), including the resurrection of those who have died. It is generally agreed that this vision portrays events during the Persian and Greek empires, particularly as they affected the Jews.

Two different perspectives

The stories and the visions are told from different perspectives. The stories are in the third person—they are told *about* Daniel; the visions are in the first person—Daniel himself relates what he has seen. Hence, in the earlier chapters the reader is given an overview of what takes place by a seemingly omniscient narrator and has access to information that no individual in the story could know; in the later chapters the reader shares Daniel's limited perspective and his limited understanding, which is emphasized several times. Indeed, in the stories Daniel is the one who is able to interpret dreams and visions, but when it comes to his own visions in the later chapters, he is unable to interpret them and needs help from a divine messenger. Perhaps, by implication, the reader also needs divine help to understand what is going on.

Two eras referred to

The setting of the stories is quite explicit: they are dated by the years of various exilic kings and are set during Israel's captivity in Babylon or Persia. Chapters 1—4 all take place within the reign of the Babylonian King Nebuchadnezzar, who reigned when Judah fell to Babylon (in 587BC). Chapter 5 is also set during the Babylonian exile, this time under King Belshazzar. However, the events of this chapter take place just before the Babylonian empire falls to the Persians (in 539BC). The king in chapter 6 is the Persian King Darius. Precise dating of this chapter is more difficult, as we will see later.

The visions are also *set* during this period (in other words, Daniel sees the visions during the reigns of the Babylonian King Belshazzar and the Persian King Cyrus), but they relate to events occurring right up to the second century BC (and, some would argue, much beyond that time). Indeed, the primary focus of these visions seems to be events that took place in the 160s BC, especially the abolition by King Antiochus IV Epiphanes, in 167BC, of a twice-daily offering performed in the temple in the morning and at dusk, and his desecration of the altar, which effectively brought to an end the Jewish temple cult. Events are described as they relate to Jerusalem, suggesting that the physical setting is back in Judah rather than in exile. Thus, while the stories clearly describe events in exile under Babylonian and Persian rule in the sixth century BC, the background to the visions seems to be Jerusalem under the persecutions of Antiochus IV Epiphanes in the second century. This may indicate that the visions were written at this time, but commentators disagree over this dating.

Two different languages

One of the strangest features of the book of Daniel is that it uses two different (although related) languages. The first chapter is in Hebrew (like most of the rest of the Old Testament). But in 2:4 we read the words, 'The Chaldeans said to the king (in Aramaic)...' and what follows is in Aramaic. When the Chaldeans finish speaking, however, the Aramaic continues, right up to the end of chapter 7. Chapters 8—12 are then in Hebrew again. Thus, chapters 1 and 8—12 are in Hebrew, while chapters 2—7 are in Aramaic, and this division cuts across the division between the stories in chapters 1—6 and the visions in chapters 7—12. But there is another feature that indicates the unity of chapters 2—7: these chapters are carefully structured in a pattern commonly used in the Old Testament, known as a chiasmus (from the Greek letter *chi*, shaped like an X):

A   Dream about four earthly kingdoms and God's kingdom (ch. 2)
   B   Story about Jews being faithful in the face of death (ch. 3)
      C   Story about royal hubris that is humbled (ch. 4)
      C   Story about royal hubris that is humbled (ch. 5)
   B   Story about Jews being faithful in the face of death (ch. 6)
A   Vision about four earthly kingdoms and God's kingdom (ch. 7)

This may indicate that chapters 2—7 circulated independently before chapters 1 and 8—12 were added. Chapter 1 does have the feel of an introduction, setting the scene and introducing the main characters. Chapters 8—12 then have a very different feel from the earlier chapters. They seem to have events of the second century BC as their background, rather than the sixth century as is the case with chapters 1—6. In some ways, chapter 7 is different from both but has clear links with both. It may be that it functions as a pivot between the earlier and the later chapters: as Lederach suggests, it has a 'dual purpose' (p. 19), concluding the Aramaic section of the book and also introducing the visions written in Hebrew.

Two canonical forms

Like the rest of the Old Testament, Daniel exists in a Hebrew form and in a Greek form (in fact, there are a number of Hebrew and Greek manuscripts). The Hebrew version lies behind the book that appears in Protestant editions of the Bible, while the Greek is used as the basis of Catholic editions. The Greek version has three additions that do not appear in the Hebrew. 'The Prayer of Azariah and the Hymn of the Three Young Men' is inserted after 3:23 and relates a prayer and hymn offered while Shadrach, Meshach and Abednego (= Azariah) were in the furnace. 'Susanna' is often found as chapter 13 of Daniel (or appears in the Apocrypha), although in some Greek manuscripts it appears before chapter 1. This is because we encounter here a very young Daniel. The story tells of a woman called Susanna who is raped by two elders of her village. It is Susanna, however, who is put on trial for adultery and would have been found guilty and executed but for the intervention of Daniel. 'Bel and the Dragon' usually occurs as the final chapter in Daniel (or in the Apocrypha). It consists of two stories in which Daniel shows the superiority of his God (and actually of himself) over the gods of King Cyrus of Persia. In the second story, Daniel is again thrown to the lions, this time for six days. While in the lions' den, he is fed by the prophet Habakkuk. In this commentary we will follow the Hebrew text and will not deal with the additions found in the Greek text.

Two places in the canon

In the Christian Old Testament, Daniel appears as the fourth of the major prophets, following Isaiah, Jeremiah and Ezekiel, and just before the twelve minor prophets. In the Hebrew Bible, the book is to be found among the Writings, following Esther and just before Ezra-Nehemiah. This may be largely because of when it was written, but there is also an impact upon its interpretation if we don't presume that it is one of the 'prophets' and instead read it as one of the 'exilic' or 'post-exilic' books. Indeed, although Daniel clearly draws extensively on Isaiah, Jeremiah and Ezekiel, it is quite different literature from these other books.

Apocalyptic literature

One of the ways in which Daniel is different from other Old Testament literature is that it contains more 'apocalyptic' material than other books. Indeed, it is regarded by many as the only Old Testament 'apocalypse', just as Revelation is the only New Testament apocalypse. The term 'apocalypse' is a somewhat slippery one, however, and there has been much debate about just how it should be defined and what should be described in this way. The term derives from the opening words of the book of Revelation: 'The *revelation* [*apocalypse*] of Jesus Christ, which God gave to show his servants what must soon take place; he made it known by sending his angel to his servant John.' It is clear that Revelation draws heavily on Daniel. There are a number of non-biblical books which are categorized as 'apocalyptic literature' (1 Enoch, 2 Enoch, 2 Apocalypse of

Baruch, 3 Apocalypse of Baruch, 4 Ezra, Apocalypse of Abraham, Apocalypse of Peter) but Daniel is also quite different from these in some ways. Therefore, Daniel is often taken as an early example of an 'apocalypse' upon which later writers drew in different ways. Nonetheless, there are earlier parts of the Old Testament which also contain material that might be described as 'apocalyptic', particularly Isaiah 24—27, Joel, the early chapters of Ezekiel and parts of Zechariah. Daniel probably drew on such works as these. Full-blown apocalyptic literature is typically characterized by:

- The expectation of an impending cosmic catastrophe
- The use of fantastic imagery to portray this end-time
- Parallels between earthly and heavenly events
- The intervention of heavenly beings: angels and demons
- Salvation beyond the catastrophe for the faithful
- A division of human history into clearly defined segments
- Pseudonymy, where the work is ascribed to an ancient biblical worthy
- Reuse of biblical imagery

Relationship to other biblical books

As we work through Daniel, it will be obvious that it draws extensively on other biblical literature. This is an important key to understanding the book: it is largely an interpretation of events in Israel's history in light of other biblical material. The most obvious parallel to the first six chapters is the story of Joseph in Genesis: there are very clear links between the two which rather suggest that the author of Daniel at least knew the Joseph stories and drew upon them as he wrote about Daniel. There are also parallels with the book of Esther, but not such as would suggest that it influenced the writing of Daniel. The final six chapters draw particularly on the major prophets (Isaiah, Jeremiah and Ezekiel), although they make use also of the minor prophets and some other parts of the Old Testament.

The message of the book

There is no doubt about the overriding message of the book of Daniel, whether in the stories or the visions, in the Hebrew chapters or in the Aramaic section: regardless of the actions of the powerful rulers of human empires, ultimate sovereignty resides with the God of the Jews and with that God alone. The implications of this message are different in different contexts. Thus, in the first six chapters, the faithful Jews cooperate as much as possible with the foreign kings and are able to function effectively within the political structures of those regimes. They do practise a degree of non-violent resistance, but they earn the respect of the kings and hold high office in the kings' court. Indeed, for the most part the kings are rather well-disposed to the faithful Jews in their court. Things are very different in the second half of the book, where foreign rulers are seen as oppressors who try to subdue the Jews and prohibit the practice of their religion. There is no hint here that it might be possible to cooperate with these regimes and certainly not to hold high office while remaining a faithful Jew. At the same time, there is no suggestion that violent resistance should be contemplated, and there may even be condemnation of those who take this route. Instead, faithful Jews are to remain true to their God and trust that God will work things out aright in the end. Indeed, they are to remain faithful even if it costs them their lives—as it will for many, it seems. At 'the time of the end' they will rise to receive their reward.

Other commentaries

Joyce G. Baldwin, *Daniel*, Tyndale Old Testament Commentaries (IVP, 1978)
An accessible commentary, although her conclusions are more conservative than mine. Good on application.

John J. Collins, *Daniel*, Hermeneia (Fortress Press, 1993)
Probably *the* recent academic commentary on Daniel. Very thorough, although a complex read at times.

P.R. Davies, *Daniel*, Old Testament Guides (JSOT Press, 1985)
An introductory book which provides an overview of the contents of the book of Daniel and outlines the main issues that engage the scholars.

John E. Goldingay, *Daniel*, Word Biblical Commentary (Word Books, 1989)
A thorough and reasonably conservative commentary which relates scholarly study of Daniel to issues of life and faith today. More accessible for those with some theological training, and some knowledge of Hebrew helps.

Paul Lederach, *Daniel*, Believers Church Bible Commentary (Herald Press, 1994)
This is one of my favourites! It tackles the scholarly issues in an accessible fashion and comes to what I consider to be reasonable conclusions on important issues, like dating of the different parts of Daniel. Each section concludes with some application for today.

Ernest C. Lucas, *Daniel*, Apollos Old Testament Commentary (Apollos, 2002)
For an up-to-date commentary that takes the scholarly questions seriously and also seeks to make some application to life and faith today, this is my first choice.

Paul L. Redditt, *Daniel*, New Century Bible Commentary (Sheffield Academic Press, 1999)
This is an accessible academic commentary which, while it does not give space to application, concludes each chapter with a section on 'theology'.

C.L. Seow, *Daniel*, Westminster Bible Companion (Westminster John Knox Press, 2003)
A fairly academic but nonetheless accessible commentary, with some application to life and faith today.

Ronald S. Wallace, *The Message of Daniel*, The Bible Speaks Today (IVP, 1979)
A conservative approach to the book of Daniel which seeks to tease out its message for Christian life today.

1

SETTING *the* SCENE

Chapter 1 of Daniel sets the scene for the whole book. The first two verses introduce the reader to the overall setting in three different ways. Verse 1, along with verse 21, establishes the time frame within which the events recorded in the book are set. Verse 2, along with verse 3, indicates the place in which they are set. Verse 2 also gives us our first taste of the overriding theme of the book, a theme that is reiterated many times in various different ways. Verses 1–2 also function as the introduction to a chiasmus, which characterizes chapter 1. Lucas outlines the pattern thus:

A Historical introduction (1:1–2)
  B The young men taken for training (1:3–7)
    C The story of the test (1:8–16)
  B The young men excel in their training (1:17–20)
A Historical conclusion (1:21)

The time frame

It must be acknowledged that the date indicated in verse 1 (probably 605BC) raises some difficulties. Jeremiah 25:1 clearly states that the first year of Nebuchadrezzar (an alternative spelling of Nebuchadnezzar) was the *fourth* year of Jehoiakim's reign, not the third as asserted here. It is possible that the discrepancy results from the different ways of calculating the years of a king's reign: sometimes the king's first year was counted as year 1, at other times as year 0. Be that as it may, the key point about the time frame is that the whole of Daniel is set in the period when a significant proportion of Israel's population was in exile.

Daniel 1:21 refers to the first year of King Cyrus. This is 539BC, the year when Cyrus issued an edict permitting the Israelites to return to their homeland. A central question in Daniel is how Israelites, or Jews as they later became known, were to remain faithful to their God in a land where their faith was a minority view. (Details about the events that took place at this time may be found in 2 Kings 24:1—25:20; 2 Chronicles 36:5–21; Jeremiah 39:1—40:6; 52:1–34.) This is an issue that remains very pertinent for Christians in many parts of the world—and to an increasing extent in the supposedly 'Christian' countries of the West.

The location

Shinar (v. 2) is another name for Babylonia. This is where the events in Daniel are set, although the use of the term 'Shinar' here may intentionally recall its use elsewhere in the Old Testament. This is especially the case in relation to Genesis 11, which relates the building of the tower of Babel. In Zechariah 5:11, at the conclusion of a vision that would not be out of place in the second half of the book of Daniel, 'wickedness' finds its home in Shinar.

The theology

The most significant aspect of these two verses is embedded in verse 2: 'The Lord let King Jehoiakim of Judah fall into his power.' In Hebrew this is, 'The Lord gave into his hand King Jehoiakim of Judah.' The Lord's *giving* is an important concept in this chapter (it reappears in verses 9 and 17 in Hebrew, although this is not obvious in the NRSV translation of verse 9, which reads, 'Now God *allowed...*'). But the theological point is crucial and provides the overriding theme of the book of Daniel: although it may seem that foreign empires control the destiny of the Israelites, it is actually the Lord who exercises the ultimate power. The Lord, the God of the Israelites, is sovereign, and even the seeming victory of the Babylonians (and later the Persians, then the Greeks, then the Romans) happens only because God permits it as part of God's own greater purposes. We should just note, however, that the covenant name of the God of the Jews ('Yahweh', usually rendered by 'the LORD' in capital letters in English Bibles) is not used in these verses. In fact, the divine name 'the LORD' is only used in chapter 9 of Daniel, and we will discuss it further at that point.

REFLECTION

The overriding message of Daniel is that ultimately God is in control, even though it sometimes doesn't feel like that. How do we cope when it seems as if wickedness has the upper hand?

EDUCATION *or* INDOCTRINATION?

In this section we are introduced to the hero of the book and three of his fellow Israelites who feature in a number of the stories in chapters 1—6. These young men were, it seems, the *crème de la crème* of the exiled Israelites: of royal stock, without defect (a requirement in Leviticus for the priesthood and also for sacrificial animals), handsome, skilled in all wisdom (the term 'skilled' is a significant one when it is translated as 'wise' in 11:33, 35; 12:3, 10), knowledgeable, insightful, competent—and the description in Hebrew is even more glowing than in English! But what is Nebuchadnezzar's purpose in educating these fine lads? Is he 'benevolent and enlightened', as one commentator argues (Wallace), or does he 'set about a process of conditioning and indoctrination' (Russell)?

Chaldean culture

There is some ambiguity about the term 'Chaldeans' (v. 4). It may simply refer to Babylonians, as seems to be the case in 5:30 and 9:1, or it may refer specifically to a category of 'wise men' (alongside magicians, enchanters and sorcerers), as it does in 2:2, 4, 5, 10; 3:8; 4:7; 5:7, 11. If it is the latter case, the young Israelite men would be trained in the arts of Babylonian magic, which would certainly sit uncomfortably with their own religion. It seems more likely, though, that they were simply educated in the literature and language of Babylon. While this is less overtly 'conditioning and indoctrination', literature and language can be very powerful tools in helping to inculcate a particular worldview. We might consider how important a nation's literature is in forming its identity, or how tenaciously countries that feel under threat of losing their identity cling to their national language: Wales provides a good example. Immersing these young people in the language and literature of Babylon was probably intended to train them to adopt a Babylonian worldview.

Educated for three years

What is true of literature and language in particular is true of education in general, and verse 5 informs us that these Jews were to be 'educated for three years' in Chaldean ways. Education is a very powerful tool, and there are innumerable ways in which the seemingly most innocuous subjects can be taught so that changes are wrought in the students' political, social or religious perspective. Education in our own country has changed massively over a short period of time. Much of this is for the good. Some of it, however, results from changes in the way our society thinks about political, social and religious matters and represents a move away from Christian values.

Given other names

Names in the Old Testament are more than just 'tags'. A name captures something important about the person to whom it is given. The names of the Israelite young men (v. 6) all relate to their God: Daniel means 'my God is judged'; Hananiah, 'the Lord has been gracious'; Mishael, 'who is what God is?' and Azariah, 'the Lord has helped'. It seems to have been common practice in Old Testament times for a conquering king to change the names of people he conquered, especially the kings. For example, we read in 2 Kings 23:34 that 'Pharaoh Neco made Eliakim son of Josiah king in place of his father Josiah, and changed his name to Jehoiakim'. So the Babylonians changed the names of these young men (v. 7), thus indicating their control over them. But this renaming also removed the allusions to the God of the Israelites and replaced them with allusions to the Babylonian god, Bel or Marduk. (It should be noted, however, that the precise meaning of the new names is unclear.) This means that, in addition to educating them in the ways of Babylon, and in particular immersing them in Babylonian literature and language, Nebuchadnezzar sought to mould the young Israelites by giving them Babylonian names containing references to the gods of Babylon. We might note that in Revelation, Christians are pictured as receiving new names (2:17); and, of course, the name of Jesus is very important in the New Testament: it is indeed the name at which every knee shall bow (Philippians 2:10).

REFLECTION

Proverbs 22:6 asserts, 'Train children in the right way, and when old, they will not stray.' In what ways might we seek to ensure that children in our society receive an appropriate education?

3

DRAWING *the* LINE

The story that these verses relate is the central part of chapter 1. It looks as though Daniel accepted Babylonian education and his name-change, both of which were ways of subjecting him to Babylonian authority. For some reason, however, he drew the line at eating the 'royal rations' (v. 8, literally 'portions of the king' in Hebrew) assigned to him. This seems strange: why take a stand over something that seems relatively minor? Commentators make a number of suggestions and many conclude that because verse 8 repeatedly refers to Daniel's unwillingness to 'defile himself', it must be something to do with Jewish food laws. This is unlikely for two reasons. First, refusing meat would eliminate the risk of eating prohibited meat or meat that wasn't prepared according to Jewish laws, but this doesn't explain Daniel's refusal to drink wine, which is not prohibited for most Jews. Second, 10:3 implies that later Daniel did eat meat and drink wine. So why does he refuse here?

Daniel's resolve

A subtle clue may be found at the start of verse 8: 'But Daniel *resolved…*' What is not apparent in English translations is that the word translated 'resolve' here is used twice in the previous verse: 'The palace master *gave* them other names: Daniel he *called* Belteshazzar…' The verb literally means 'put, place, set', but may be rendered by a range of English words depending on the context. The point is that in the previous verse a servant of the king decided what Daniel should do, but in this verse Daniel decides what is right—what he considers will 'defile' him in God's eyes. It may be that, in the end, the food itself was relatively unimportant. What was important was that Daniel refused to allow the king to control his life completely because his allegiance was to a higher authority—his God. The eventual result was that when Daniel and his three friends outshone the others, it wasn't because of the king but because these men acted as they believed God would want, and God honoured their action.

God's giving

We noted earlier that the Hebrew of 1:2 says, 'The Lord *gave* into his hand King Jehoiakim of Judah'. In verse 9 we read, 'God *gave* Daniel favour and compassion in the eyes of the palace master', which indicates God's active involvement in events at critical points—even if this involvement would not be obvious to the people concerned. This is the faith perspective of Daniel: despite appearances, it is not the Babylonian king or his minions who control events, but God who is ultimately in control. We find this viewpoint elsewhere in the Old Testament. For example, in the events of Joseph's life, God features little but is nonetheless shown clearly to be in control; similarly, in the book of Esther, God seems to be working in the background—even though God is not mentioned at all.

Whom do you 'fear'?

In verse 10 the palace master says, 'I am afraid of my lord the king' (and note that 'my lord' is the same word used of God in 1:2). He goes on to express his fear that allowing Daniel not to eat the royal rations might 'endanger my head with the king'. The palace master fears the king, in the sense of being afraid of him. This is contrasted with Daniel's 'fear' of God in the sense of appropriate reverence. The Hebrew word, just like the English 'fear', can have both senses. A key theme in Daniel is the contrast between the 'fearful' ruling powers and a 'fearful' God. Twice in chapter 10 Daniel is told not to fear in the sense of being afraid, but throughout the book he demonstrates that he has an appropriate fear, or reverence, of God. This fear of God proves justified: when the palace master agrees to a ten-day trial of very simple food for Daniel and his friends (vv. 11–15), they end up being much healthier than their peers. It is unlikely that this was simply because of the food. Rather, it appears that again the God whom they feared gave them their success.

REFLECTION

There is much in society that would 'control' us, and there is a real danger in acquiescing. Just like Daniel, we need to maintain aspects of our lives that are distinctive and indicate where our ultimate allegiance lies. Pray that God will show you where you should draw the line, and will give you an understanding of others who take their stand in different ways.

4

DANIEL 1:17–21

KNOWLEDGE, WISDOM & INSIGHT

The concluding verses of chapter 1 pick up in significant ways on the early verses, bringing a certain roundness to the chapter. In particular, the story related in the preceding verses is brought to a conclusion by the reference to the 'knowledge', 'wisdom' and 'insight' of the four young men (v. 17), first mentioned in 1:4. Also, Nebuchadnezzar's 'flexing his muscles' is further indicated by the emphatic use of 'brought' twice in verse 18, picking up on its use in 1:2–3. Finally, the date in verse 21 is important, reflecting back to 1:1.

God's giving again

The section opens with the third reference in this chapter to God's giving. Here 'God *gave* knowledge and skill in every aspect of literature and wisdom', and 'Daniel also had insight...' This picks up on 1:4, where the young men were 'versed in every branch of wisdom' and 'endowed with knowledge and insight'. The difference is very significant, although the two verses need not contradict each other. The earlier verses show no indication that these were God-given abilities, but in verse 17 it is made quite explicit. That is to say, ultimately it is God who is responsible for these gifts, and certainly not the foreign king or his 'education'. Thus, while the emphatic use of 'brought' twice in verse 18 (in Hebrew the two occurrences of the word appear together in the middle of the verse) describes the Babylonians' power to move people around at will, the passage again indicates that ultimately it is God who controls events. Nonetheless, although these were God-given gifts, the young men had the responsibility of using them wisely—both in serving God and in being effective courtiers in the foreign court. In both realms, it seems, they shone. The effective and wise use of God-given gifts for specifically religious purposes and in service of other people is very important.

Daniel's 'mantic' wisdom

The last part of verse 17 serves to introduce Daniel's special abilities, which will be a major feature of his role in the rest of the book: 'Daniel also had insight into all visions and dreams.' This is a different kind of wisdom from what is found in the Wisdom literature in

28

the Old Testament (Job, Proverbs and Ecclesiastes). In this literature we find didactic wisdom (which teaches people how to live well in the world God created) and reflective wisdom (which reflects upon God's world, especially the difficulties that that world throws up). The predominant form of wisdom in Daniel is what is known as 'mantic' wisdom, which is described here as 'insight into all visions and dreams'. Such wisdom was a feature of Babylonian and particularly Persian society, so, to function effectively among the wise men of those societies, Daniel also needed to be skilled in this way. Indeed, verses 18–20 indicate that Daniel and his friends outdid the local talent at their own game! In Genesis we find Joseph displaying similar skills.

A book for 'exile'

Chapter 1:1 dates the start of the book of Daniel to the beginning of the exile. Verse 21 describes Daniel functioning within the Babylonian royal court up to the time of Cyrus, the Persian, who permitted exiled Israelites to return to their homeland. This probably isn't intended to suggest that Daniel either died at this time (although he would already have been an old man), or returned to Israel (see 6:28 and 10:1). Rather, it indicates that Daniel was a prophet of the exile. This is important because the book of Daniel continues to speak powerfully to those who are experiencing some kind of 'exile'. Some scholars (notably Brueggemann) argue that Christians in the West today are effectively in exile in a foreign land, and, of course, the same would be true in other parts of the world.

Like Daniel and his friends, we should acknowledge the ultimate source of the things God has given us and strive to use them as best we can for religious purposes and to serve other people, even if those people do not share our faith, and even if we feel like exiles living in a foreign land.

REFLECTION

What has God given you? Give God thanks for these things and ask his help to put them to best possible use.

On INTERPRETING DREAMS

In the introduction, we noted that there is a chiastic structure to chapters 2—7, such that chapter 2 has some significant links with chapter 7. In looking at this passage, we should also recall that in verse 4 there is a change from Hebrew to Aramaic. Continuing from chapter 1, chapter 2 starts in Hebrew, but after the words, 'The Chaldeans said to the king (in Aramaic)', the text changes to Aramaic, which then continues through to the end of chapter 7.

On difficulties with dates

Again there is some difficulty over the date given in verse 1, and especially how it correlates with the previous chapter. Chapter 1 mentions three years' training for the young Jewish men, all within Nebuchadnezzar's reign; chapter 2 seems to assume that such training is now completed and that Daniel is to be counted among 'the wise men of Babylon', but it is set 'in the second year of Nebuchadnezzar'. While there is a variety of scholarly opinion on the matter, my view is that the dates in Daniel are not intended to give historical precision, but are indicative of something. In this case, verse 1 indicates that the chapter is describing the next significant thing to occur near the start of Nebuchadnezzar's reign.

Portrait of a tyrant?

It is often claimed that Nebuchadnezzar is presented in quite a positive light in Daniel. I think that is true to some extent, but this passage does cast him as something of an unreasonable tyrant. This figure of supreme authority in Babylon demands the impossible from his advisers; God, the true supreme authority, readily provides what is sought to his faithful servant Daniel. The contrast between human sovereigns and God is key in Daniel.

The dream and its interpretation

Dreams and their interpretation were important in the ancient Near East, and there are various records of the dreams of kings (like the Babylonian king Nabonidus, of whom we'll hear more in discussion of ch. 4). In the Old Testament, Pharaoh's dream in Genesis 41 provides the closest parallel, and this is another of many links between the Joseph story and Daniel. Notably, King Nebuchadnezzar always links the dream and its interpretation (the two words occur together when he mentions them in vv. 6–7), while his wise men try to separate them (illustrated by the fact that in their speech the words never occur together). For most of us, this emphasis on dreams seems strange—it is not a way we often (if ever) expect God to speak to us. Actually, it was not the main way in which God was understood to speak in the ancient Near East, either, but it was one way nonetheless.

Revelation

What is really significant in this chapter is not so much the dream, or even its interpretation, but the fact that *God* could reveal its interpretation. Indeed, the word translated 'interpretation' (which occurs once in the Old Testament outside Daniel) includes the sense of interpretation by supernatural revelation (see Lucas, p. 63). Later in chapter 2 there is a specific word for 'revelation'; here there is repeated emphasis (seven times) on 'declaring the interpretation' of the dream. It is significant that the Chaldeans say, 'There is no one on earth who can reveal (actually "declare") what the king demands', and 'no one can reveal ("declare") it to the king except the gods, whose dwelling is not with mortals' (vv. 10–11). The task is beyond the impressive human resources of the king of Babylon, and his gods are too remote to help. Daniel, as we shall see, has recourse to a much more intimate God who will 'declare' to him what he needs to know.

Christianity is a 'revealed' faith: the 'interpretation' of human life is 'declared' to us primarily through Jesus, in very important ways through the Bible, but also in other ways. Such interpretation is beyond the very impressive capacities of human reasoning. Think about what aspects of your faith require something more than purely human resources.

REFLECTION

At various points in the Bible, God reveals something through dreams (although there are also cautions about dreams). Would we be ready to hear if God communicated with us in this way?

6   DANIEL 2:13-19

The MYSTERY REVEALED

The problem has been established in the earlier verses of this chapter (the wise men of Babylon are to be killed because no one can tell the king his dream and interpret it for him): now 'Daniel and his companions' (v. 13) are reintroduced because they are to be killed along with the other wise men. In verse 17, the companions' Hebrew names are used; this is a bit strange because their Babylonian names appear at the end of the chapter. This is one reason why some scholars suggest that verses 13–23 did not originally belong with this chapter. They also argue that Daniel's appearance before the king in verse 16 does not fit with verses 24–30. Nor does his request for time in verse 16 fit with the king's response to the other wise men when they stall for time in verse 8. In addition, it is pointed out that the narrative flows well if verses 13–23 are omitted. There is certainly a difficulty here, although various explanations have been offered. I shall deal with the text as we have it, whatever happened before it reached this final form.

Prudence and discretion

Facing execution, Daniel does not panic. Nor, it seems, does he immediately look for a miraculous escape. Daniel may have been gifted with 'insight into all visions and dreams' (1:17), but his first recourse is to human (if, perhaps, 'sanctified') wisdom (as exemplified in the Old Testament Wisdom literature): he acts 'with prudence and discretion' (v. 14). Moreover, his concern is down-to-earth and also displays a generous spirit: he seeks to save the lives of his friends and himself, and the lives of 'the rest of the wise men of Babylon'. Daniel first gets his facts straight (by speaking to Arioch, the king's chief executioner); he then goes to the king (probably a very brave thing to do) to try to buy some time (v. 16); and only then does he do 'the spiritual bit'. He may, of course, have prayed straight away, but we're not told as much. Sometimes we need simply to act wisely rather than looking for a 'spiritual' answer.

Time for prayer

The next step is some serious prayer. Daniel seeks out other trusted friends and asks them to pray (vv. 17–18). What they pray for is God's mercy, but specifically in relation to the issue they faced—a 'mystery' (v. 19) whose incomprehensibility looked like being, quite literally, the death of them. The word translated 'mystery' is a Persian term which occurs only in Daniel in the Old Testament (in this chapter and once more in 4:9). Towner observes, 'Its exact sense is something of a mystery itself' (p. 32), but its use in Daniel implies a mystery that can only be resolved by divine help.

Mystery is an important element of faith, and it may be that the Wisdom books of Job and Ecclesiastes are, among other things, warnings that God is mysterious and beyond our understanding. The New Testament also refers quite often to the mystery of faith, which needs to be revealed to us: for example, Colossians 1:26 speaks of 'the mystery that has been hidden throughout the ages and generations but has now been revealed to his saints'. While faithful Christian living is often about acting 'wisely', faith also involves an acceptance of the 'mysterious', which is beyond human wisdom.

Revelation

The text doesn't state how quickly 'the mystery was revealed'; it may have been as soon as the Jews started praying. Anyway, 'revelation' was the answer to their prayer. The word used here means to 'uncover, expose'. The Aramaic word occurs only in this chapter in Daniel (vv. 19, 22, 28, 29, 30, 47), and twice in Ezra, but the Hebrew word is common elsewhere in the Old Testament. The observation that God reveals mysteries is, as we shall see, a key theme in the rest of chapter 2.

REFLECTION

Think about your own Christian life. When do you need simply to act wisely rather than looking for a 'spiritual' answer? When do you face 'mysteries' whose solution only comes about by God's help? Pray for wisdom to know the difference and how to act appropriately.

DANIEL'S PRAYER

When (as soon as?) Daniel's prayer is answered, he responds with a hymn of praise to God. The language of this hymn is similar to parts of the book of Psalms and also bears some similarities to passages in Job (see, for example, Job 1:21; 12:22; 32:8; 38:19). A number of commentators refer to these verses as a doxology (a hymn ascribing glory to God) and point out that there are similar doxologies in Daniel 2:47; 4:1–3, 34–37; and 6:25–27. We also find doxologies at key points in the Psalms (41:13; 72:18–19; 89:52; 106:48; 150). Redditt classes this hymn in Daniel as 'a three-verse doxology (vv. 20–22) followed by an individual song of thanksgiving' (p. 55). This makes sense, because the first three verses are more general praise of God, while the final verse thanks God for what he has done for Daniel in this specific case. Seow sees these verses as the theological pivot around which the whole chapter revolves. He states, 'His prayer provides the theological premise upon which the following account depends' (p. 41).

Blessing

Blessing God is an important aspect of Christian worship. We often bless God in song (for example, in the song, 'Blessed be the name of the Lord'); many of us bless God before we eat (sometimes referred to as 'giving the blessing'); we may bless God in prayer (as, for example, when we conclude a prayer with 'Blessed be Father, Son and Holy Spirit'). But we may do this without giving much thought to just what we're doing. Lederach usefully explains: 'To bless is to empower; when used toward God, it means to give thanks, honor, and appreciation to the one named' (p. 62). This is what Daniel does when God answers his prayer. He opens his thanksgiving psalm, or doxology, by blessing God (v. 20), then he relates some of the things God does (vv. 21–22). Finally, he specifically gives thanks for what God has revealed to him (v. 23). In fact, he blesses God for the revelation with which God blessed him.

Wisdom and power

The key theme of these verses (and an important theme throughout the chapter) is emphasized by being used as an *inclusio*, which means that it occurs near the start and again near the end, like bookcovers enclosing a book. This key theme is 'wisdom and power'. The prayer makes clear that ultimately wisdom and power reside with God, and God decides who receives such wisdom and power. Thus, in verse 20 we read that 'wisdom and power are his' (that is, God's), then in verse 23 Daniel thanks and praises God because 'you have given me wisdom and power'. In this chapter the Babylonian king clearly is powerful and he has access to many wise men, but his power and wisdom have been shown to be limited. It is the wisdom and power that come from God which really count in the end.

Revelation, again!

The theme of God's revelation continues to be an important one. Daniel notes that God 'reveals deep and hidden things' (v. 22), using darkness as symbolic of hidden things, and light as a way of expressing God's revelation. He then gives God thanks because God has 'now revealed to me what I asked of you, for you have revealed to us what the king ordered' (v. 23). This ties in Daniel's hymn quite specifically with the events of chapter 2. It should be noted, though, that a different verb (literally 'to know') is used in verse 23 both times where the NRSV says 'revealed'. We thus have three words represented by 'reveal' in the NRSV—'declare', 'expose or uncover' and 'know'—which convey different aspects of what the English word 'reveal' means.

REFLECTION

Think about how you respond to answered prayer: consider how readily you thank God and praise God for the answers you receive. Ask yourself how much your prayers focus on who God is as well as focusing on specific situations (though it must be said that there are times for 'arrow' prayers which often amount to 'Help!').

8

A GOD *who* REVEALS MYSTERIES

The narrative here picks up well from verse 12, and we may recall how some scholars suggest that verses 13–23 are a later addition. One reason for this suggestion is that Arioch's words, 'I have found among the exiles from Judah a man who can tell the king the interpretation', seem to indicate that the king had not met Daniel before. Whether these scholars are correct or not, in the text as we now have it, 2:13–23 prepares well for this passage because it shows how Daniel responded to the king's threat to destroy 'all the wise men of Babylon', and how he received the interpretation of the king's dream. We are also given important insight into the kind of God that Daniel worships, especially, of course, that this God is one who 'reveals deep and hidden things' (2:22). Thus we gain significant information about Daniel and God. The verse immediately preceding our section informs us that Daniel received wisdom and power from God, as well as the revelation of the dream's interpretation. We now see Daniel acting with wisdom.

Wisdom

Daniel chooses carefully his route to the king: he goes through Arioch 'whom the king had appointed to destroy the wise men of Babylon' (v. 24). The implications of this are that Daniel is introduced to the king by the very person appointed to kill him, who may well have had good reason for not wanting to carry out the king's command. This course of action also buys Daniel a little more time by distracting the executioner for a while; Daniel specifically says to him, 'Do not destroy the wise men of Babylon', as if that is just what he was on his way to do. Daniel states that he will 'give the king the interpretation', and thus implies that he knows the dream as well. However, the king still quite specifically asks, 'Are you able to tell me the dream that I have seen and its interpretation?' (v. 26).

Revealing mysteries

Daniel's response picks up on the words spoken by the Babylonian wise men when they said, 'There is no one on earth who can reveal (remember that the word is actually "declare") what the king demands... no one can reveal ("declare") it to the king except the gods, whose dwelling is not with mortals' (2:10–11). Daniel agrees that this is beyond any human capacity (v. 27); he also agrees that a god can reveal it (and the word here is specifically 'reveal'). The God Daniel has in mind, however, is not like the remote Babylonian gods; not only is Daniel's God able to reveal such mysteries, this God has actually done so. This is emphasized here by repetition: in verse 28 Daniel states, 'There is a God in heaven who reveals mysteries', and in verse 29 he affirms that 'the revealer of mysteries disclosed to you what is to be'.

Giving glory to God

A very significant aspect of this passage is Daniel's refusal to take the glory for telling the king his dream and its interpretation. This stands in sharp contrast to the Babylonian wise men who had said, 'Tell your servants the dream, and *we* will reveal ("declare") the interpretation' (2:4). When the king asks Daniel, 'Are *you* able to tell me the dream that I have seen and its interpretation?' he first responds, '*No* wise men, enchanters, magicians, or diviners can show to the king the mystery that the king is asking.' But then he goes on to affirm that 'there is a God in heaven who reveals mysteries, and he has disclosed to King Nebuchadnezzar what will happen'. Here we find another similarity with the Joseph story, where we read, 'Pharaoh said to Joseph, "I have had a dream, and there is no one who can interpret it. I have heard it said of you that when you hear a dream you can interpret it." Joseph answered Pharaoh, "It is not I; God will give Pharaoh a favourable answer"' (Genesis 41:15–16).

Daniel is successful where all the Babylonian wise men had failed, but he doesn't take the credit for it personally. In the previous section, we saw Daniel ascribing his wisdom and power, as well as the revelation, to God. Most of us like to be successful. We're not always so good at giving God the credit for our success. It's not wrong to be proud of the good things we do, so long as we appreciate that ultimately it is God who enables us to do them.

REFLECTION

Think about how well you balance taking personal pride in things you do with giving God the glory for those things. Pray for God's help to achieve a good balance.

NEBUCHADNEZZAR'S DREAM

The dream and its interpretation in this chapter are the most 'apocalyptic' elements of chapters 1 to 6. In this respect they fit well with the second half of the book (hence some scholars suggest that they are a later addition in this context)—especially with chapter 7. The dream contains a rather strange picture, which is then interpreted to reveal forthcoming events in world history. This is not unusual in ancient dreams (again, think of Pharaoh's dream in Genesis 41, where cows and ears of grain represent years of plenty and years of famine). Daniel's interpretation also tells of a decisive eschatological (end-time) action by God some time in the future: this is characteristic of apocalyptic material.

A huge statue

The dream opens with the words, 'You were looking, O king, and lo!' (v. 31). Similar words appear at the beginning of Daniel's vision in 7:2, only in the first person rather than the second person as here (and similar words also appear in 4:10). Then immediately a huge statue is described, which was extraordinarily splendid and frightening. Collins states that 'apparitions of gigantic figures are characteristic of ancient Near Eastern dreams' (p. 162), so this element of the dream would not have been unusual. What is unusual is that the statue represents eras in history rather than a god, as is usual elsewhere. It also paves the way for the gigantic statue (with measurements provided) that features in chapter 3.

It is interesting to note that the Aramaic word used for 'statue' here is the same Hebrew word that appears in Genesis 1:27 for people being created in God's image. It seems that just as a statue represents something (often a god in the ancient world), so we too are created to be God's 'representatives' on earth.

Gold, silver, bronze, iron and clay

Most scholars argue that the quality of the materials diminishes as they move down the statue. That is to say, its head is the best bit (v. 32); then it gets worse and worse until we reach the 'feet of clay' (a mixture of iron and clay, actually) in verse 33. Collins points out that there are other examples in ancient literature of history being represented by 'a sequence of metals of declining value' (p. 162). The best-known of these is found in *Works and Days* by the eighth-century BC Greek writer, Hesiod. At any rate, this great, splendid and frightening statue is actually very vulnerable because of its feet of clay. Indeed, impressive, awe-inspiring human creations or institutions often (or always?) have their weak spots where they are actually very vulnerable, and may be brought down surprisingly quickly (and ultimately by God). This has certainly been true of great empires of the past, and may well be true of the materialistic society in which we find ourselves in the Western world today. It is worth noting that 'feet of clay' has passed into common English usage, even though many who use the phrase have never heard of Daniel.

A stone not made by human hands

The stone which was not made by human hands (v. 34) does not have parallels in other ancient literature. It is rather strange and clearly represents something to do with God. While the statue was vulnerable because of its feet of clay, the action of this stone is extraordinary: it not only brings the statue down, but also causes it to be completely demolished so that no trace of it is left (v. 35). Moreover, this stone then 'became a great mountain and filled the whole earth'. The concept of 'the Lord's mountain' is an important one elsewhere in the Old Testament (for example, Isaiah 2:2–4). Moreover, in the New Testament we find Jesus depicted as a chosen and precious cornerstone and 'a stone that makes [people who disobey the word] stumble and a rock that makes them fall' (1 Peter 2:8).

REFLECTION

Do you think you have 'feet of clay', and if so, can you identify what they are? Pray for all those who have such 'feet of clay', including, perhaps, those aspects of our society that might make it vulnerable to collapse in the future.

The INTERPRETATION

We mentioned *inclusio* earlier: we have a further example here. Reference to 'the dream' and 'its interpretation' form an *inclusio* round this section (and these references don't appear at all in between the 'bookends'):

v. 36   This was *the dream*; now we will tell the king *its interpretation*.
v. 45   *The dream* is certain, and *its interpretation* trustworthy.

There may also be a chiasmus, including the above *inclusio* and references to God's interaction with the king:

A This was the dream; now we will tell the king its interpretation.
   B You, O king, the king of kings
      C to whom the God of heaven has given the kingdom…
         [D *interpretation of the dream]*
      C The great God has informed
   B the king what shall be hereafter.
A The dream is certain, and its interpretation trustworthy.

As indicated above, the interpretation of the dream sits in the middle of this chiasmus, with B and C leading into it, and C and B bringing it to a conclusion.

The statue

There is some dispute among scholars over exactly what the statue represents. There are those who hold that because the head is explicitly interpreted as Nebuchadnezzar (v. 38), the rest of the statue also represents a succession of kings. We should note that the oft-repeated word 'kingdom' might equally be rendered 'kingship' or 'reign', and most scholars see the various parts of the statue as representing various empires. The majority understand the four empires to be Babylonian, Median, Persian and Greek, and this seems to me to be most probable. I suspect that the text was written in the Greek period when that part of the empire that affected the Jews was split between Ptolemaic and Seleucid rulers (of which more later), and that this is what is represented by the feet 'partly of potter's clay and partly of iron'. However, there is a long-standing

Christian tradition that sees the four kingdoms as Babylonian, Medo-Persian, Greek and Roman (see Baldwin, pp. 65–68). This view is often held by those who argue for an exilic date for Daniel and maintain that the book contains largely predictive prophecy. It is also associated with prophecy about Jesus, who is, for example, linked to the 'stone not made by human hands' in this passage. It is probably wisest not to be too concerned about the precise interpretation of the various bits of the statue. What is of more significance is that the statue, whatever precisely it represents, is destroyed by the 'stone not made by human hands'.

The extraordinary stone

Again, however, there is disagreement among scholars concerning the precise identity of the kingdom represented by the stone. Thus, for example, Wallace says, 'Of the meaning of the stone we can be in no doubt. Christ's is the kingdom *cut from a mountain by no human hand*' (p. 58). On the other hand, Redditt states that 'the kingdom in question is Israel or a subgroup thereof' (p. 60). Actually, it is possible, and in my view likely, that both could be right! Thus Lederach states, 'The stone represents the kingdom of God or the rule of God' (p. 70). In the time when this part of Daniel was written, that description probably referred to faithful Jewish believers. For us it is quite appropriate to see it as a reference to the kingdom of God inaugurated by Jesus, whereby God's rule is seen through Christ's Church. This is very important because it means that a text which meant one thing for its original readers can legitimately be extended to refer to something beyond their time and comprehension. The writer did not, in my opinion, intend a reference to the Church; nonetheless, as we reflect on the text in light of Christ, we see that it does now include the Church. Even within the Old Testament itself, texts are reused in different circumstances as people see how the truths they convey can have relevance for a later time.

REFLECTION

How do you respond to the uncertainty we have observed
in the precise interpretation of scripture? How do you respond
to the overall message of the passage, that God has established
a kingdom that will rise above all other kingdoms
and will never come to an end?

GOD of GODS & LORD of KINGS

With this section, chapter 2 draws to a close and the scene is set for the events of chapter 3. The conflict in this chapter has not really been between Nebuchadnezzar and Daniel, or the Babylonian wise men and Daniel (or Nebuchadnezzar and all the wise men); the implicit conflict has been between the gods represented by Nebuchadnezzar and his wise men and the God of Daniel. Thus, in 2:11, we read the response of the Babylonian wise men to Nebuchadnezzar's demand: 'The thing that the king is asking is too difficult, and no one can reveal it to the king except the gods, whose dwelling is not with mortals.' This is contrasted with Daniel's response: 'There is a God in heaven who reveals mysteries, and he has disclosed to King Nebuchadnezzar what will happen at the end of days' (2:28). In this respect, the theme of the chapter is similar to a key theme in Isaiah 40—55 (usually known by scholars as 'Second Isaiah'): the Lord is God of gods; all other gods are worthless, if, indeed, they exist at all.

Nebuchadnezzar's worship

The climax of the chapter arrives when Nebuchadnezzar acknowledges Daniel's God, employing the term that Daniel used earlier, 'revealer of mysteries': 'Truly, your God is God of gods and Lord of kings and a revealer of mysteries, for you have been able to reveal this mystery!' (v. 47). This probably doesn't mean that Nebuchadnezzar converted to Judaism as such; it is more likely that he added Daniel's God to the gods he already worshipped. Nonetheless, we see here the great and powerful king of Babylon acknowledging that Daniel's God is indeed a God above all heavenly and earthly authorities.

There is one aspect of this passage that has often troubled readers: King Nebuchadnezzar first worships Daniel (v. 46). Scholars explain this in a variety of ways, but many presume that Daniel (like Paul and Barnabas at Lystra in Acts 14:11–18) refused to receive such worship; however, the text simply does not say. It may well be that Nebuchadnezzar's response was not the one the Jews would have hoped for; nonetheless he did repent and acknowledge and worship God.

Daniel's reward

These verses depict Daniel being richly rewarded for his service to the king and his obedience to God (v. 48). Such a conclusion is not unusual in the Old Testament, and again reminds us of Joseph. We need, of course, to be careful not to read here a theology which states that service of God will always result in material blessing. Such is certainly not the case. Daniel might have been tempted to gloat over his promotion above the other wise men, but his hymn earlier in the chapter suggests that he would not have yielded to the temptation: there he ascribed 'wisdom and power' to God and thanked God for giving him 'wisdom and power'. This was none of Daniel's doing; ultimately these events were in the hands of God.

Daniel's friends reappear

The final verse (v. 49) achieves two things. First, it demonstrates that Daniel was not simply thinking of himself, but considered also his three friends (who presumably would further the Jewish influence within the Babylonian government structures). The verse also reintroduces the three friends (this time by their Babylonian names) in preparation for the events in chapter 3.

Giving glory to God

Throughout this chapter we see Daniel acting with wisdom and integrity. He displays common sense, discretion and great courage. He thinks not only of himself but also of his friends and, indeed, of all the wise men of Babylon. Moreover, in everything he gives glory to God. The result is that the most powerful man of the moment saw God at work through Daniel and acknowledged God.

PRAYER

Sovereign God, help us to live in such a way that our actions demonstrate you at work in our lives. May other people see something of you through us.

12 DANIEL 3:1-7

The GOLDEN STATUE

We have met the concept of 'chiasmus' before, and we may have another example of this kind of literary pattern in chapter 3. Lucas proposes the following structure:

A Nebuchadnezzar's decree to worship the golden image (3:1-7)
  B The Jews accused (3:8-12)
    C The Jews threatened (3:13-15)
      D The Jews confess their faith (3:16-18)
    C The Jews punished (3:19-23)
  B The Jews vindicated (3:24-27)
A Nebuchadnezzar's decree honouring the Jews and their God (3:28-30)

If this is correct, it has important implications for interpretation of the chapter because it places the Jews' confession of their faith and their refusal to engage in inappropriate worship right at the centre of the chapter.

A further significant literary feature of this chapter is the large amount of repetition within it. In verses 1-7 the phrase 'the statue that King Nebuchadnezzar had set up' is heavily emphasized by its use five times following the opening words, 'King Nebuchadnezzar made a golden statue'. In the next section (3:8-12) we find the words 'the golden statue that *you* set up' addressed to the king by 'certain Chaldeans'. In the following section, Nebuchadnezzar himself refers to 'the golden statue that *I* have set up' (3:14). We then return to 'the golden statue that *you* set up' in the next passage (3:18), after which it is not mentioned again.

The 'setting up' of the golden statue is contrasted with 'falling down to worship', also repeated. The list of Babylonian officials is repeated, perhaps in a mocking way—that is, to show that all these high officials mindlessly respond like automatons to Nebuchadnezzar's command to worship the statue. A similar effect may be achieved by the repetition of 'peoples, nations and languages', and of the list of musical instruments, and again by the focus on the fiery furnace later in the chapter. Shadrach, Meshach and Abednego's names are emphasized by repetition (when in most cases the pronoun 'they' would have sufficed) 13 times.

A rather grotesque image?

The statue is very large (about 30 metres high) and contains a large quantity of gold, even if, as many commentators suggest, it is overlaid with gold rather than being made of solid gold. It isn't clear whether it is a statue of a god or of Nebuchadnezzar himself. Either way, the constant emphasis on 'the statue that King Nebuchadnezzar had set up' clearly indicates that it is closely associated with the king and is a sign of his power. The dimensions are strange, however: its proportions are 10:1 (height to width), while normal human proportions are around 5:1 or 6:1. This means that the statue would have been rather grotesque because of its elongation, which may be part of the writer's attempt to mock Nebuchadnezzar and his command to worship this object.

The centrality of worship

There seems to be another chiasmus running from the end of verse 3 through to verse 7:

A the statue that King Nebuchadnezzar had set up
  B peoples, nations and languages
    C horn, pipe, lyre, trigon, harp, drum and entire musical ensemble
      D fall down and worship
      D fall down and worship
    C horn, pipe, lyre, trigon, harp, drum and entire musical ensemble
  B peoples, nations and languages
A the golden statue that King Nebuchadnezzar had set up

This chiasmus places worship at the centre, and, indeed, the centrality of *appropriate* worship is emphasized in this chapter.

REFLECTION

The literary features of this chapter emphasize the central importance of 'falling down in worship'. How would you describe 'appropriate worship' and how important should it be for a Christian?

13

SHADRACH, MESHACH & ABEDNEGO

These verses pick up on the repetition in 3:4–7 and play out an important reversal of what is depicted there. In 3:4 and 5 a command was issued, then in verse 7 the obedience of 'all the peoples, nations and languages' was described using very similar language (with some minor variations in Aramaic).

This portrays the people's obedience 'to the letter' (or almost, at least). It is picked up again in verse 10 with very similar wording. However, while in 3:7 we read that 'all the peoples, nations and languages fell down and worshipped the golden statue that King Nebuchadnezzar had set up', this time Nebuchadnezzar is told of Shadrach, Meshach and Abednego that 'they do not worship the golden statue that you have set up' (v. 12).

'Certain' Chaldeans and 'certain' Jews

A contrast is drawn here between 'certain Chaldeans' (v. 8) and 'certain Jews' (v. 12). The Aramaic word translated 'certain' occurs only in chapter 3 in Daniel and literally means 'men' (it is used again of the 'three men' in 3:24 and the 'four men' in 3:25). Goldingay points out, 'The three who were merely *youths* in chap. 1 and merely Daniel's *friends* in chap. 2 are here full-grown *men* of importance in their own right' (p. 70). As noted earlier, there is a lot of emphasis placed on Shadrach, Meshach and Abednego because their names are repeated many times in the rest of the chapter. Notably, there is no mention of Daniel here whatsoever. In light of the statement at the end of chapter 2 that the king 'appointed Shadrach, Meshach, and Abednego over the affairs of the province of Babylon', it seems likely that the Chaldeans were acting out of jealousy because the Jews had been promoted over them. At this stage, the three men are not being persecuted purely on the basis of their Jewishness—although they are being required to break the first two of the Ten Commandments.

Who or what will we worship?

The first part of the Ten Commandments states that we should have no gods other than the Lord, or idols, and that we should not bow down to worship such things (Exodus 20:3–5). Whether the golden statue represented a god or Nebuchadnezzar himself, it is clear that it would have been inappropriate for a Jew to worship it. The Chaldeans' statement, 'They do not serve your gods' (v. 12) gives a good indication that the issue wasn't simply about bowing down to a statue of Nebuchadnezzar: in the end, Shadrach, Meshach and Abednego had to decide whether or not to worship the gods of the people among whom they were living, and would have to suffer the consequences if they decided not to.

Presumably Shadrach, Meshach and Abednego could have melted into the crowd and acted in such a way that they didn't stand out. They might even have convinced themselves that they weren't doing anything wrong, but were simply avoiding unnecessary conflict. Indeed, it looks as though they would not have been found out if it hadn't been for the jealousy of the Chaldeans over whom they'd been promoted. People in high office are very susceptible to being picked up on the slightest thing they do, if it doesn't fit in with other people's priorities. Christians in such positions especially need our prayer and other support.

In this country we may not often be persecuted specifically on the basis of our faith. Even so, a refusal to 'worship' the 'gods' of the people round about us is likely eventually to bring conflict, and may result in persecution.

REFLECTION

What are the 'gods' of our society, and what constitutes 'worship' of them? How might Christians avoid getting caught up in it?

The GOD *that* WILL DELIVER YOU?

Again in this section repetition of key phrases from the earlier passages is used to good effect. Nebuchadnezzar's words in verse 15, 'Now if you are ready when you hear the sound of the horn, pipe, lyre, trigon, harp, drum, and entire musical ensemble to fall down and worship the statue that I have made, well and good. But if you do not worship, you shall immediately be thrown into a furnace of blazing fire', repeat much of what we find in 3:5 and 10.

In 3:5 the king's command was issued for the first time. In 3:10 it was reiterated by 'certain Chaldeans' as they tried to get 'certain Jews' (Shadrach, Meshach and Abednego) into trouble. Now King Nebuchadnezzar reissues his edict directly to Shadrach, Meshach and Abednego to find out for himself if they will obey. This serves to place considerable emphasis on the king's command and builds up to the inevitable confrontation between Nebuchadnezzar and these Jews. Already at this point the king is 'in furious rage' (v. 13); by the time the three men have responded to him, his rage is so great that 'his face was distorted' (3:19). A further repetition also points forward to the climax of this confrontation in the next section. In 3:12, the Chaldeans accused the Jews to Nebuchadnezzar, saying, '*They* do not serve your gods and *they* do not worship the golden statue that you have set up.' In verse 14 the king asks them directly, 'Is it true, O Shadrach, Meshach, and Abednego, that *you* do not serve my gods and *you* do not worship the golden statue that I have set up?' Then in 3:18 the Jews affirm, '*We* will not serve your gods and *we* will not worship the golden statue that you have set up.'

'If' and 'if not'

The reference three times in each section (3:1–7, 8–12, 13–15) to 'worship' indicates again the centrality of worship in this story. In the first section, everyone was commanded to worship and told the consequences if they did not. 'All the peoples, nations and languages' then fall down and worship. In the second section we discover that, in fact, not 'all the peoples, nations and languages' fell down and worshipped, because Shadrach, Meshach and Abednego did not worship as they were commanded. In this third section Nebuchadnezzar gives the Jews a straight choice: if you are ready to worship, well and good, but if not, you shall immediately be thrown into a furnace of blazing fire. Shadrach, Meshach and Abednego are faced with either engaging in inappropriate worship or heading for what looks like certain death. As we will see later, they respond by issuing their own 'if' and 'if not', which stand in sharp contrast to what the king says here.

Who is the God?

The true nature of the conflict comes across at the end of verse 15, where Nebuchadnezzar in his arrogance asks, 'Who is the god that will deliver you out of my hands?' Although Shadrach, Meshach and Abednego are mentioned often in this chapter, they are actually minor characters in the drama that is worked out. The main characters are Nebuchadnezzar (and his gods) and the God of the Jews. Although this God doesn't feature explicitly very often, as the chapter develops it becomes clear that the God of Shadrach, Meshach and Abednego is constantly there in the background, and that it is this God who has control over events and not the seemingly all-powerful Nebuchadnezzar (or his gods). The whole chapter so far has been building up to the inevitability that Shadrach, Meshach and Abednego will go to the 'furnace of blazing fire' because they will worship no other god but their own God. The climax arrives with this question, which also prompts the only words that the three Jews speak. With the speech in which they make clear that they will only serve their God, the pivot around which the chapter revolves is reached.

The king's question might be reworded for our own context: 'Who is the god that will deliver us from the challenges we face?' I wonder what, in the end, we truly rely on for our security. Is our trust really in God, or do we 'buy in' to the security our society relies on—job security, financial security, and so on? Would we stick by our trust in God even if it cost us such security… even to the point of death, if necessary?

PRAYER

Sovereign God, give courage to those for whom openly worshipping you brings considerable danger, perhaps even the risk of death.

NO COMPROMISE!

These verses convey the only recorded words of Shadrach, Meshach and Abednego in the chapter. Moreover, this section constitutes the centre of the story around which the whole plot revolves. The repetition in the earlier verses has been building up to this point, and with their words here these Jewish men seal their fate: hot on the heels, so to speak, of what they say to Nebuchadnezzar, he gets ready the 'furnace of blazing fire' and has them thrown into it.

No need to present a 'defence'

Shadrach, Meshach and Abednego's words could be read as very insulting to the king. For a start, to address the king as simply 'O Nebuchadnezzar' (v. 16), without using any title, forms something of a contrast to the words of the Chaldeans in 3:9: 'O king, live forever!' (They speak in exactly the same way in 2:4, and the 'presidents and satraps' address Darius with the words, 'O King Darius, live forever!' in 6:6.) This is probably the author's way of contrasting the attitude of these Jewish men, who are resolute in their determination to worship none other than their God, with others who appear to obey Nebuchadnezzar's command to worship the golden statue without a second thought. Then, secondly, to say, 'We have no need to present a defence to you in this matter' could be read as a statement of defiance along the lines of 'we don't need to justify ourselves to you'. The Aramaic doesn't use a word for 'defence' here, however; it simply says, 'We have no need to return to you on this matter.' This might mean that they didn't feel the need to explain their refusal to obey or, more probably, it refers back to what immediately precedes this verse—Nebuchadnezzar's question in 3:15, 'Who is the god that will deliver you out of my hands?' Rather than refusing to explain their stance, the three Jews will not seek to speak on God's behalf: as the following verses make clear, deliverance is in God's hands, not theirs or Nebuchadnezzar's.

'If' and 'if not' again

These verses have been the focus of much disagreement. The problem of the conditional 'If our God whom we serve is able to deliver us' has long been noted. Many translators and commentators, from ancient times up to today, are unhappy with the implication that Shadrach, Meshach and Abednego doubt whether, in fact, God is able to deliver them. A comparison of different modern English versions reveals different approaches to this issue:

> *If we are thrown into the blazing furnace, the God we serve is able to save us from it, and he will rescue us from your hand, O king.* (NIV)

> *If that is the case, our God whom we serve is able to deliver us from the burning fiery furnace, and He will deliver us from your hand, O king.* (NKJV)

> *If our God whom we serve is able to deliver us from the furnace of blazing fire and out of your hand, O king, let him deliver us.* (NRSV)

In the first two cases, no doubt is expressed about God's ability to deliver the Jews. Although the NRSV's reading is the most difficult theologically, it is the one that most accurately renders the Aramaic. This reading also provides the best counterbalance to Nebuchadnezzar's 'if' and 'if not' in the previous section. Whether this constitutes a 'theoretical possibility that God will not intervene' (Goldingay, p. 71) or real doubt on the part of Shadrach, Meshach and Abednego is difficult to assess. I rather suspect it is the latter.

This is where the 'if not' part in verse 18 comes in: if God delivers them, great (whether or not they are confident that God can deliver them); but even if God does not deliver them, they will still refuse to worship Nebuchadnezzar's gods and his statue. These men will not compromise their religious principles regardless of the circumstances in which they find themselves, and they refuse to hold God to ransom: they will worship God and God alone, whatever happens. In this way, the text is relevant to the many Christians who do not experience God's deliverance from their dreadful circumstances, and gives them hope that they can experience God's presence with them even in the worst of situations.

REFLECTION

*If the Jews here express some doubt about God's ability
to deliver them, this also is true to many people's experience:
they cling on to faith in God even when they are not fully convinced
that he can save them.*

The Appearance of a God

In this section, good use is again made of repetition to enhance the impact of the text. Shadrach, Meshach and Abednego have featured throughout the last three sections, but the focus on them here is highlighted by the fact that they are named four times in verses 19–23. After that point, they are just the 'three men' as attention shifts to the fourth man in the fire. Also in verses 19–23 there is a heavy emphasis on the furnace. First we are told that Nebuchadnezzar 'ordered the furnace to be heated up seven times more than was customary', then 'the furnace of blazing fire' is mentioned three more times, 'the furnace' once, 'the raging flames' once and the fact that it was 'overheated' once. In addition, of course, its heat is so great that it kills the guards who throw the Jewish men into the furnace. In verses 24 and 25, however, it is just 'the fire': the great heat is no longer relevant. The unnecessarily hot furnace is accompanied by the extremity of the king's rage, which distorted his face (v. 19), the great strength of the guards (v. 20), and the excessive clothing worn by the Jewish men (v. 21). Usually people would be stripped of their clothes before being thrown into a fire. It is also mentioned four times that the men are bound, which builds up to the observation in verse 25 that there are now four men in the fire, who are all unbound.

There is a play on words in verse 19 that is lost in translation. The Aramaic says something along the lines of 'the "image" of his face was changed', and the word 'image' is the word that is used earlier of the statue that Nebuchadnezzar had set up. This play on words may hint that the statue was, in fact, a representation of Nebuchadnezzar rather than of a god. At any rate, the Jews' refusal to worship the statue sent the king into a blazing fury.

A prayer and a hymn

In the Greek Old Testament (the Septuagint) and in the Catholic Bible there are an extra 66 verses slotted in between verses 23 and 24. The first two verses read, 'They walked around in the midst of the flames, singing hymns to God and blessing the Lord. Then Azariah stood still in the fire and prayed aloud', and there follow 20 verses in which Azariah offers a prayer to God. This is followed by a short narrative that includes the information, 'the angel of the Lord came down into the furnace to be with Azariah and his companions, and drove the fiery flame out of the furnace'. Finally, all three Jews 'with one voice praised and glorified and blessed God in the furnace' with a hymn that appears in the Church of England's Book of Common Prayer and *Common Worship* as the 'Benedicite' or 'a Song of Creation'. It seems likely that these verses constitute a late addition to Daniel, and they do rather disrupt the flow of the chapter. They are therefore omitted from Protestant Bibles.

The fourth man in the furnace

Verses 24 and 25 constitute the turning point in the story. It has been building up to the point where Shadrach, Meshach and Abednego are thrown into the furnace to face what seems like certain death. Now comes the twist: Nebuchadnezzar observes that not only are the three men walking round unbound and unharmed in the midst of the fire, but they have been joined by a fourth who 'has the appearance of a god'. The text doesn't reveal who this enigmatic person is, except that Nebuchadnezzar describes him as God's angel in 3:28. It should be noted, however, that this is Nebuchadnezzar's understanding of the situation and not a statement by the author of the book. Chapter 6 may provide a parallel, when Daniel says that it was an angel who shut the lions' mouths. In Christian tradition, the fourth person here has been identified with Christ.

It is often pointed out that the real significance of this passage is that God doesn't prevent the three men from being thrown into the fire, but comes to them in it. Similarly, when Christians today face periods of suffering, God does not always prevent that suffering: it is the testimony of many, though, that God has come to be with them in a special way at such times. The form of this coming varies, and sometimes is hard to pin down. Thus, although the text does not present the fourth person as Jesus, nonetheless it might be appropriate to refer to him as 'Immanuel', God with us, a name used in connection with Jesus in Matthew 1:23.

PRAYER

Sovereign God, may those who face suffering today know you with them in that suffering. May your presence give them comfort and strength to endure.

BLESSED BE GOD

This final section of chapter 3 has a number of links with the beginning of the chapter. For a start, verse 27 picks up on the repeated list of officials in 3:2 and 3, although the list is abbreviated here and occurs only once—thus the emphasis achieved in the earlier verses is absent. Also in the opening section, reference to 'peoples, nations and languages' is repeated: in this final section it too occurs just once (v. 29). Notably, however, the oft-repeated reference to 'the (golden) statue that King Nebuchadnezzar had set up' does not feature at all here: it has disappeared from view. This connects with the fact that both these passages describe decrees issued by the king. At the start of the chapter he decrees that everyone will worship his statue. Now he decrees, 'Any people, nation, or language that utters blasphemy against the God of Shadrach, Meshach, and Abednego shall be torn limb from limb, and their houses laid in ruins; for there is no other god who is able to deliver in this way.' The focus has shifted from Nebuchadnezzar and his statue to Shadrach, Meshach and Abednego and their God.

The Most High God

After the emphasis on the furnace and its great heat in the previous section, this passage shows clearly that even so hot a furnace has no power whatever over Shadrach, Meshach and Abednego. Nebuchadnezzar approaches the door of 'the furnace of blazing fire' (v. 26), then the Jews come 'out from the fire' completely unscathed. All the king's officials see that 'the fire had not had any power over the bodies of those men' and that 'not even the smell of fire came from them' (v. 27).

The focus moves from the furnace, which 'had not had any power' over the Jews, to the God who not only had power over these men but also over the natural elements. This God is first described by Nebuchadnezzar as 'the Most High God' (v. 26), an expression that occurs throughout chapter 4 and a few times in chapters 5 and 7. This probably does not indicate that the king had converted to Judaism, but rather that he saw the Jews' God as the most powerful God, who should occupy an appropriate place among the pantheon of Babylonian gods.

Nebuchadnezzar twice refers to this God as 'the God of Shadrach, Meshach and Abednego' and once as 'their own God'. He also twice refers to these Jews as 'servants' of this God. It is clear that the way these men conducted themselves and the trust they put in their God, even in desperate straits, had a big impact on the king. Hence he notes (with approval!) that they had disobeyed his command and were prepared to die 'rather than serve and worship any god except their own God' (v. 28). He rewards them by promoting them 'in the province of Babylon' (v. 30).

Nebuchadnezzar's confession

The climax of the chapter is the king's statement: 'Blessed be the God of Shadrach, Meshach, and Abednego, who has sent his angel and delivered his servants who trusted in him.' Moreover, when he says here that 'there is no other god who is able to deliver in this way', he provides the answer to his own (rhetorical?) question in 3:15: 'Who is the god that will deliver you out of my hands?' This is a significant turnaround indeed! It does not prevent us from being shocked, however, at the harshness of his final decree: such a threat is hardly how we would wish to encourage people to worship God.

We noted earlier the emphasis in the early part of this chapter on appropriate worship. The chapter returns to this theme at the end. The key phrase here is 'rather than serve and worship any god except their own God'. Shadrach, Meshach and Abednego flatly refused to engage in such worship, even when their lives were in severe danger for doing so. Their stance had made the king furious, but eventually, when God intervened, Nebuchadnezzar came to see the power of God and responded in worship. Compromising our faith often seems the easiest way forward and may well avoid arousing anger and generating conflict. On the other hand, sticking uncompromisingly to our beliefs not only maintains our integrity, but it may eventually bring people round as they see the impact of God upon our lives.

REFLECTION

What is your experience either of compromising or of refusing to compromise your faith under pressure from other people? How do you reflect on that in light of the story described in this chapter?

18

NEBUCHADNEZZAR PRAISES GOD

This section starts with a puzzle: the beginning of chapter 4 in English translations is the end of chapter 3 in Aramaic. The question then arises as to whether this paean of praise fits best at the end of the account of the fiery furnace, or at the beginning of the story of the king's second dream. For three reasons, I think the English translations have got it right here. Firstly, chapter 3 finishes in similar fashion to chapter 2: both have Nebuchadnezzar praising the God of the Jews in words that tie in with the key theme of the chapter, and both conclude with the Jewish men being promoted. Chapter 4 follows a similar pattern, except that at the end of this chapter Nebuchadnezzar is restored to his position of authority rather than the Jews being promoted. Each chapter can be seen to pick up on the previous one and shows development in Nebuchadnezzar's understanding of the God of the Jews.

Secondly, King Nebuchadnezzar's praise of God at the start and end of the chapter form something of an *inclusio* round the material that comes in between, especially the references to God's kingdom and sovereignty:

> *His kingdom is an everlasting kingdom, and his sovereignty is from generation to generation* (4:3).
> *His sovereignty is an everlasting sovereignty, and his kingdom endures from generation to generation* (4:34).

Indeed, the contrast between Nebuchadnezzar's sovereignty and God's sovereignty is the key theme in the chapter, just as God 'revealing mysteries' is the key theme in chapter 2, and God 'delivering his servants who trusted in him' is the key theme in chapter 3.

Thirdly, as Lederach explains, Nebuchadnezzar's letter 'follows a common form, with 4:1–4 providing a typical introduction, 4:5–33 making up the body of the letter, and 4:34–37 forming the conclusion' (p. 91). The fact that this letter is addressed to 'all peoples, nations, and languages that live throughout the earth' indicates Nebuchadnezzar's understanding of the importance of his own sovereignty. This contrasts with his acknowledgment at the end of the chapter of 'the King of heaven' who 'is able to bring low those who walk in pride' (v. 37).

The king and Daniel

Redditt (p. 76) proposes the following chiastic structure to the chapter, which, if he is correct, would provide further support for the chapter division in English translations.

4:1–3: Prologue. Proclamation. Doxology 1
   4:4–6: Dream reception by king
      4:7–9: Instructions: king to Daniel
         4:10–17: Dream recital: king to Daniel
            4:18–19: Dialogue: king and Daniel
         4:20–26: Dream interpretation: Daniel to king
      4:27: Instructions: Daniel to king
   4:28–33: Dream fulfilment upon king
4:34–37: Epilogue. Restoration. Doxology 2

This places at the centre of the passage the handover of control from Nebuchadnezzar to Daniel and, by implication, to Daniel's God. At this point the perspective of the narrative changes: it is in the first person up to this point, with the king himself relating what had happened to him, but from here until the epilogue it changes to third person, with the king's experience being described by someone else—either Daniel or the narrator. This captures in a literary way Nebuchadnezzar's loss of control or sovereignty.

Acknowledging God's sovereignty

In this chapter, the writer employs 'shock tactics' to emphasize the principal theme of the chapter: it starts with the most powerful ruler of the time—a foreigner and not an adherent of the Jewish faith—acknowledging the sovereignty of Daniel's God. It seems that at last, after several striking encounters with God, Nebuchadnezzar has come to the point where he acknowledges God's sovereignty over his own. As we meet Nebuchadnezzar for the last time in chapter 4, we find that he now very readily offers praise to God: 'The signs and wonders that the Most High God has worked for me I am pleased to recount' (v. 2).

REFLECTION

Think about what led you to 'encounter God' (if indeed that has happened). How readily do you relate the experience to others?

19

WHERE REAL SOVEREIGNTY
RESIDES

These verses at the start of chapter 4 introduce some key words, which are repeated several times throughout the chapter, helping to convey its main emphasis.

Earth and heaven

The contrast between earthly sovereignty and God's sovereignty features throughout the chapter in the repetition of the word 'earth' nine times and 'heaven' 15 times, although it is not always obvious in English translations. This contrast is a key theme throughout the book of Daniel even when it is not explicitly addressed. Thus, for example, it is a crucial element in the way the final vision of the book in chapters 10—12 is to be interpreted, even though the issue is not directly raised. In chapter 4 itself, it is notable that the chapter opens with a reference to 'all peoples, nations, and languages that live throughout the earth' (v. 1), and closes with a description of 'the King of heaven' (4:37), the only time this expression is used for God. Moreover, close to the end of the chapter it is stated that 'all the inhabitants of the earth are accounted as nothing' (4:35), and the turnaround for King Nebuchadnezzar comes when he 'lifted [his] eyes to heaven' (4:34).

The Most High God

The expression 'Most High' to describe God is used more in this chapter than anywhere else (most notably in the 'refrain', which we will consider briefly below). This correlates with the exaltation of God's sovereignty and the humbling of Nebuchadnezzar, who was the most high of all earthly rulers. The words 'Most High (God)' on Nebuchadnezzar's lips indicate that he acknowledges Daniel's God as having greater authority or sovereignty than any other god. The same words on Daniel's lips refer to the only God, the Lord. The equivalent Hebrew term, *el elyon* (or just *elyon*), occurs often in the Old Testament in reference to the Lord.

Great and mighty

The words 'great' and 'mighty' in verse 3 are used to describe what God does (in this instance, God's 'signs and wonders', which elsewhere in the Old Testament usually refer to God's actions against the Egyptians, when the Israelites under Moses were liberated from their bondage in Egypt). Elsewhere in the chapter they are used of Nebuchadnezzar and his deeds (4:11, 20, 22, 30), which are shown not to compare with God's 'signs and wonders'.

Kingdom/sovereignty

We noted in the previous section that the *inclusio* enclosing this chapter emphasizes the key theme of God's kingdom and sovereignty, as opposed to the earthly kingdom and sovereignty of Nebuchadnezzar. This theme appears throughout the chapter, and is particularly noteworthy in a 'refrain' in verses 17, 25 and 32: '… that all who live may know that the Most High is sovereign over the kingdom of mortals; he gives it to whom he will'.

This refrain is picked up again in chapter 5, where Daniel recalls to Belshazzar what happened to his 'father' Nebuchadnezzar: '… until he learned that the Most High God has sovereignty over the kingdom of mortals, and sets over it whomsoever he will' (5:21).

The refrain indicates not only that sovereignty ultimately belongs to 'the Most High God', but also that it is God who determines who reigns on earth.

For the first readers of Daniel, it must at times have seemed difficult to believe that their God really was sovereign when it was so obvious that their lives were controlled by foreign earthly rulers. It is sometimes (or often?) difficult for us to believe it, too.

REFLECTION

What helps you to hold on to belief in God's ultimate sovereignty
even when ungodly forces seem to control your destiny,
at least in the short term?

DANIEL CONSULTED AGAIN

This section reminds us of chapter 2: here again Nebuchadnezzar is troubled by a dream and seeks an interpretation from his wise men. This time, however, the king at least deigns to tell the wise men what the dream is. Nonetheless, they are unable to provide the interpretation, and it is again left up to Daniel to tell the king what it is all about.

Living at ease

It seems, from verse 4, where Nebuchadnezzar says, 'I was living at ease in my home and prospering in my palace' (and again from 4:30), that life was good for Nebuchadnezzar. The first term, 'at ease', suggests a carefree, indeed a careless posture. The Aramaic word is related to the one used for blasphemy in 3:29 and for criminal negligence in 6:4 (see also Ezra 4:22). So the text implies that Nebuchadnezzar was, at best, negligent. I am reminded of the very telling verse at the start of the story of David and Bathsheba, which states, 'In the spring of the year, the time when kings go out to battle... David remained at Jerusalem' (2 Samuel 11:1). David, it seems, was at ease when he should have been leading his army—and disaster resulted. The second term, 'prospering', as Seow explains, 'is used elsewhere of the luxuriance of plants, and so one may understand the text to suggest that Nebuchadnezzar was "luxuriating in his palace"' (p. 66).

A disturbing dream

It is often when people get too comfortable with, or complacent in, the life that they have built up for themselves that disaster strikes. In David's case, the repercussions of his actions were immense for him, his family and for the nation as a whole, to say nothing of Bathsheba and the family of her husband, Uriah, whom David had killed. In Nebuchadnezzar's case, God intervenes with a dream, and the king seems to have sensed that it was of divine origin because he was deeply disturbed by it (v. 5). This is emphasized by the use of three different terms for the dream ('dream', 'fantasies in bed' and 'visions of my head') and two references to the king's fear ('frightened me' and 'terrified me').

A spirit of the holy god(s)

The king, it seems, has learned from past experience. He knows that Daniel is to be trusted when it comes to dream interpretation. Why Daniel appears after the other wise men (v. 8) is not clear, but when Daniel does eventually arrive Nebuchadnezzar is confident that he can interpret the dream because Daniel is 'endowed with a spirit of the holy gods'. This point is emphasized by its repetition here, in verse 9 and again in verse 18 (and again in 5:11, 14). The term 'spirit of the holy gods' is ambiguous: in Aramaic the word for 'gods' is plural and would have been understood as a reference to the plurality of gods found in Babylonian religion; however, the Hebrew equivalent, which is also grammatically plural, is likewise used to refer to the gods of other nations but also to the one God of Jewish faith. Either way, Nebuchadnezzar perceived that Daniel received divine help in his dream interpretation, just as Pharaoh had concluded earlier about Joseph when he said of him, 'Can we find anyone else like this—one in whom is the spirit of God?' (Genesis 41:38).

Perhaps the most dangerous time spiritually, both for individuals and for societies, is when we become comfortable and complacent. When we are 'at ease' and 'prosperous', when we fail to realize our need for God, when we think we can do whatever we want in our own strength, then it is that we may become estranged from God—sometimes without even realizing that it is happening. At such times we either need God to speak to us directly (perhaps in a vision), or for someone especially endowed with the spirit of the holy God to convey God's voice to us.

PRAYER

Sovereign God, when we live in relative security and comfort, help us not to become complacent but to continue to hear your voice.

21

ANOTHER DREAM

The dream in these verses falls into two sections (vv. 10–12, 13–17), both of which start with reference to 'visions of my head' that Nebuchadnezzar saw. These words are much more similar in Aramaic than they appear in the NRSV, and both pick up on the line in verse 5, 'my fantasies in bed and the visions of my head terrified me'. To show the similarities, the verses might be rendered literally thus:

> *Visions of my head in my bed I saw* (v. 10)
> *I saw visions of my head in my bed* (v. 13)

The whole dream then builds up to the refrain with which it concludes in verse 17, '… in order that all who live may know that the Most High is sovereign over the kingdom of mortals; he gives it to whom he will and sets over it the lowliest of human beings'.

The great and mighty tree

Elsewhere in the Old Testament, trees feature as important metaphors. The tree of the knowledge of good and evil and the tree of life in Genesis 2 and 3 are obvious examples, but the metaphorical use of trees in Ezekiel 17 and 31 is particularly relevant. In Ezekiel 17, Israel is portrayed as a twig, planted by God, that grows to be a mighty cedar, while the picture of Assyria as a mighty cedar tree in Ezekiel 31 is even more interesting: 'it towered high above all the trees of the field', and 'all the birds of the air made their nests in its boughs; under its branches all the animals of the field gave birth to their young; and in its shade all great nations lived' (31:5–6). A few verses later, however, the Lord says of it, 'Because it towered high and set its top among the clouds, and its heart was proud of its height… I have cast it out. Foreigners from the most terrible of the nations have cut it down and left it' (31:10–12).

Trees were a common motif in the mythology of ancient civilizations, where, as Goldingay states, 'A lofty, pre-eminent, verdant, protective, fruitful, long-lived tree is a common symbol for the living, transcendent, life-giving, sustaining Cosmos or Reality or Deity itself' (p. 87). The tree here in Daniel 4, which stands 'at the centre of the earth' (v. 10), whose 'top reached to heaven' (v. 11), which was 'visible to the ends of the whole earth' (v. 11), which 'provided food for all'

(v. 12) and from which 'all living beings were fed' (v. 12) is clearly a tree of cosmic proportions.

Watchers and holy ones

The word used for 'watcher' in verses 13 and 17 (also 4:23) is used in this way only in this passage in the Old Testament, although it is more common in later literature (particularly the 'Book of the Watchers' in 1 Enoch 1—36, which is a pseudepigraphical book—a later book written in the name of a biblical worthy). The fact that the 'watcher' comes 'down from heaven' (vv. 13, 23), and the link with 'the holy ones' (v. 17), suggest that the word here is effectively a synonym for 'angel'. 'Holy ones' feature often in chapter 7.

Living like an animal

The second half of the dream starts by describing the great and mighty cosmic tree being chopped down at the command of the holy watcher. In the following verse, however, leaving 'its stump and roots in the ground' (v. 15) suggests that there is still some hope for regrowth in the future. The next line, 'with a band of iron and bronze', is a mystery. It may refer to a band being applied to the stump, but what its purpose would be is unclear, and there is no evidence that such a procedure was carried out in Babylon. Perhaps it should be linked to what follows and taken to indicate the tethering of an animal. Either way, the picture shifts as the metaphor of the felled tree is left behind and the focus turns instead to a person who lives among the animals and is given the mind of an animal (v. 16) for 'seven times'—probably a symbolic way of saying 'for a long time' or perhaps specifying seven years.

Like the earlier dream of Nebuchadnezzar, this one seems very strange to us. The interpretation follows shortly, but some indication of its meaning is already given in the refrain in verse 17. The issue is again God's sovereignty. This correlates with the overriding message of Daniel, but does raise difficult questions about why God allows (or even institutes) decidedly ungodly regimes, and how citizens within such regimes should act. Throughout Daniel we see various models of both obedience to such regimes and also appropriate defiance.

PRAYER

Sovereign God, help us to know the right time for obedience to the authorities and the right time for appropriate defiance.

DANIEL'S DISTRESS

As we noted earlier, this section is the middle of the chapter, which might indicate that it is particularly important (the centre of a passage or narrative in Hebrew/Aramaic is often pivotal). The importance of this section lies in the handover of narrative control from Nebuchadnezzar to the narrator and to Daniel (speaking on God's behalf). Up to this point, everything in the chapter has been from Nebuchadnezzar's perspective, and he has effectively 'called the shots'. From this point on (until the final part of the chapter, where he again praises Daniel's God), we see things from a different angle. After the narrator has introduced Daniel, the dream is explained by Daniel, presumably giving God's perspective. The narrator then relates the fulfilment of what is predicted in the dream—the humbling of Nebuchadnezzar by 'the Most High'. Only after this is Nebuchadnezzar 'allowed' to speak again; and then it is to acknowledge the sovereignty of 'the Most High' who, the king says, 'is able to bring low those who walk in pride' (4:37).

A spirit of the holy god(s)

Once again Nebuchadnezzar acknowledges that Daniel is 'endowed with a spirit of the holy gods' (v. 18). He admits that 'all the wise men of *my* kingdom are unable to tell me the interpretation', but has confidence that Daniel, who represents another, divine kingdom, can interpret the dream for him. This is the difference between Daniel and the other wise men; it is not his greater wisdom as such, nor that he happens to be particularly good at interpreting dreams, but rather that he is 'endowed with a spirit of the holy gods'— which, we noted above, could be understood by Jews to mean a spirit of their holy God. The significance of this is that Daniel here is functioning as God's mouthpiece, so that the words we hear him speak are really God's words to Nebuchadnezzar. Thus, as Towner says, 'The real focus and center of this story is Nebuchadnezzar himself; here even Daniel lacks personality and character and functions merely as a conduit for the message of the Most High. In this sense, it can be said the real protagonists of this narrative are two sovereigns, one in heaven and one in Babylon' (p. 59).

Severely distressed and terrified

The reason why Daniel is so distressed (v. 19) is not given. It may simply be that he is to give very bad news to the most powerful of all human rulers—a ruler, moreover, who had in the past condemned people to death for much less. Ever the diplomat, Daniel tries to take some of the sting out of his explanation of the dream by telling Nebuchadnezzar that he wishes that the coming message might be applied to the king's enemies rather than the king himself. Nonetheless, he tells the king straight the interpretation he believes God has given him.

The word translated 'severely distressed' in the NRSV occurs once more in Daniel (in Hebrew rather than Aramaic), in 8:27, where again Daniel is distressed ('dismayed' in the NRSV) by a vision that this time he does not understand. The word the narrator uses of Daniel here in verse 19, that 'his thoughts *terrified* him', is repeated by Nebuchadnezzar when he says to Daniel, 'Do not let the dream or the interpretation *terrify* you', and is used by the king of himself earlier in the chapter: 'I saw a dream that frightened me; my fantasies in bed and the visions of my head *terrified* me' (4:5). This business of God's revelation through dreams and visions seems to be a pretty scary thing!

Daniel's fear and ours

Verse 19 strongly emphasizes Daniel's fear. It looks as though he had a quite natural human reaction to a terrifying situation: he was to say something very difficult to the king of the most powerful empire in the world, who might well take his life for it—and he was very afraid. How often do we shy away from saying the difficult thing, even though we believe it is the right thing to say—and with much less to lose by it than our lives! Daniel functions here as God's mouthpiece and delivers clearly and sensitively what God gave him to say, despite the risk to himself. Sometimes we too need to serve as God's mouthpiece, saying what needs to be said even if it does seem a fearful ordeal to do it. Often, actually, it is something difficult that needs to be said to a friend or fellow church member, and it may be fear of losing their friendship that holds us back.

PRAYER

Sovereign God, give us both Daniel's courage and his sensitivity to speak clearly the things you give us to say.

HEAVEN IS SOVEREIGN

In this section Daniel reiterates most of the dream in almost identical words to those used by Nebuchadnezzar, but a few bits of the dream as the king described it are missed out in Daniel's retelling (most of 4:10, 14, 16 and the start of 4:17), and these lines do not feature at all in the interpretation that Daniel gives. The details of the dream as described by Daniel are then all specifically interpreted, with two exceptions. The first is the command to 'Cut down the tree and destroy it' in verse 23; however, the interpretation of this is implicit in 'You shall be driven away from human society' (v. 25) and what follows. The second is the puzzling line, 'with a band of iron and bronze' (v. 23), which is simply left hanging without any interpretation.

The king's greatness

The first part of the interpretation (v. 22) emphasizes the king's greatness. The words used earlier of God's signs and wonders, 'great' and 'mighty' (4:3), are here applied to Nebuchadnezzar. The phrase in the NRSV, 'your greatness has increased', is literally 'your greatness has become greater', using two more forms of the word 'great' which appears earlier in the verse. The king's greatness 'reaches to heaven', which is God's realm, and his sovereignty extends to 'the ends of the earth'. Just like the cosmic tree of the dream, so Nebuchadnezzar is shown to be very great and mighty.

The king's humiliation

The king's greatness serves also to emphasize the extent of his fall. The cutting down of the tree is not specifically related to Nebuchadnezzar. Rather, the interpretation moves on to describe what will actually happen to him: he shall be driven from human society; he shall live with the animals and eat grass like they do; and he shall live under the open sky (and hence be 'bathed with the dew of heaven', v. 25). This effectively shows that the great and mighty king will be 'cut down to size'.

The refrain again

Daniel's interpretation of the dream ends on a hopeful note, however: just as, in the dream, the stump and the root were left, giving the possibility of new growth, so Nebuchadnezzar's kingdom will be re-established. But this will only happen once the words of the refrain are fulfilled: these things will continue 'until you have learned that the Most High has sovereignty over the kingdom of mortals, and gives it to whom he will' (v. 25; see also 4:17). It seems rather surprising that the last line of this refrain in 4:17, 'and sets over it the lowliest of human beings', is not picked up explicitly in the interpretation (as it is at the very end of the chapter), because a key element in the interpretation is the humbling of the mighty Nebuchadnezzar. Perhaps, though, it is picked up in verse 26 in the words 'from the time you learn that Heaven is sovereign'. Here, heaven is used as a synonym for God (the only time this happens in the Old Testament, although it is common in the expression 'the kingdom of heaven' in place of 'the kingdom of God' in Matthew's Gospel), and it shows that the great Babylonian king will at last acknowledge the sovereignty of God rather than glory-ing in his own kingship.

Daniel's advice

Having given Nebuchadnezzar the interpretation of the dream, Daniel then goes on to offer him advice. NRSV's 'atone' (v. 27) may not be the best translation here: rather, Daniel implores the king to 'break away' from his sins and his iniquities. What he is called to instead is 'right-eousness' (or 'justice') and 'mercy to the poor'; that is to say, Nebuchadnezzar is to demonstrate his humility by the way he treats those often regarded as the lowest members of society. Nebuchadnezzar was undoubtedly a very great king. Babylon was the great superpower of the time, and Nebuchadnezzar was the top man in that mighty empire. But his greatness cuts no ice with God. What matters for God, it seems, is firstly an acknowledgment that 'the Most High has sovereignty over the kingdom of mortals, and gives it to whom he will' (4:17) and secondly, sovereignty characterized by justice and mercy.

REFLECTION

What counts as greatness in our society, do you think? For Christians, greatness includes a humble acknowledgment of God's ultimate sovereignty and a concern for justice and mercy.

The DREAM FULFILLED

As often elsewhere in this book, repetition is used here to good effect. It serves to emphasize that the dream is fulfilled exactly as Daniel described in the previous section: 'All *this* came upon King Nebuchadnezzar' (v. 28). In 4:10–17 Nebuchadnezzar relates his dream; this is picked up in 4:20–26, where Daniel retells the dream and indicates pretty much point-for-point how it will be fulfilled. Then, in this section, Daniel's interpretation is picked up again twice. The first time, 'a voice came from heaven' (v. 31) to reiterate what Daniel had told Nebuchadnezzar; then the second time the narrator describes the fulfilment of these words.

The king's pride

It rather looks as though Nebuchadnezzar, despite his terror when he had the dream, and in spite of his efforts to get the dream interpreted, did not pay a great deal of attention to the interpretation Daniel provided, or to his advice. A year on (v. 29), he is still full of pride in the greatness of the kingdom he has built (v. 30). His attention on this occasion focuses on the city of Babylon itself, although, as Lederach points out, 'the city was not constructed by Nebuchadnezzar himself but by the sweat of slaves, by oppression, injustice, and exploitation of the poor' (p. 99) (so, not much sign of the justice and mercy that Daniel called for). The words 'magnificent' (used to describe Babylon) and 'mighty' (describing Nebuchadnezzar's power by which he claims to have built the city as his capital) are the same words as 'great' and 'mighty' used to describe God's signs and wonders in 4:3, the tree in the dream in 4:11 and 20, and Nebuchadnezzar himself in 4:22. The new expression, 'for my glorious majesty' (v. 30), makes it very clear that this impressive city was a source of considerable personal pride. This pride sparks off an immediate response from God.

The king's humiliation again

God's response, in the form of 'a voice [that] came from heaven' (v. 31), is to tell Nebuchadnezzar that this great kingdom has been taken away from him. According to Jeremiah 27:5–7, it was God who had given kingdoms into Nebuchadnezzar's control in the first place.

Here in Daniel 4, Nebuchadnezzar is to be humbled and the kingdoms taken from him. The voice goes on to reiterate almost word for word the interpretation that Daniel offered of the king's dream. Then immediately the dream is fulfilled, and it seems that the king suffered a period of madness, separated from the rest of society.

The need for patience

Perhaps with the passing of time Nebuchadnezzar became complacent. He was, after all, the most powerful of all kings and had succeeded in building this magnificent city that stretched out before him as he strolled around his palace rooftop. He may have thought, what could really go wrong? Maybe Daniel's God had changed his mind? Maybe his God wasn't so powerful after all? Maybe Daniel had got the interpretation wrong on this occasion? When we believe that God has spoken to us (by whatever means—directly by his Spirit, through a dream, through a word of prophecy, through a trusted friend, through the Bible, or whatever), but the word we heard seems not to take effect, it is very easy to start doubting that we heard God speak at all. All kinds of questions may spring up in our minds. It is easy also to fall back on what we know and to rely on our own devices rather than trusting God. Fulfilment of God's word to us may well be delayed, and we may never know what the reason for such delay is.

PRAYER

Sovereign God, give us discernment to hear your word, and patience when we need to wait for your word to us to be fulfilled.

NEBUCHADNEZZAR'S CONFESSION

The narrative returns now to the first person as we hear again Nebuchadnezzar's own voice. In the middle of the chapter there was a switch from first person (Nebuchadnezzar speaking as 'I') to third person address (as the narrator and Daniel took over and spoke about the king), which was possibly a literary indication that control had been removed from the king. Now control is returned to him, just as the kingdom is returned to him. As Nebuchadnezzar's speech here indicates, however, his attitude to his rule has changed as a result of what he has experienced: he now acknowledges that his sovereignty is a lesser sovereignty than that of Daniel's God.

'I lifted my eyes to heaven'

Nebuchadnezzar's response is not dramatic, simply a lifting of his eyes to heaven, but as Seow suggests, 'Perhaps that heavenward gaze was an implicit acknowledgment of the creature's neediness and dependence on divine help, indeed, from the one who watches over Israel' (p. 72). Scholars debate whether Nebuchadnezzar 'converted' to the Jewish faith. It seems unlikely that he did, but rather that he acknowledged the Jewish God as one among a number of gods he worshipped. What is significant, however, is that he realizes his 'creatureliness', acknowledging by his glance heavenward that he needed help from God or the gods. No longer did he see himself as the great and mighty king whose sovereignty was above all other sovereignty. Truly he had been humbled and brought to recognize that even the greatest king on earth was, in the end, but a creature who ultimately relied on the Creator.

Everlasting sovereignty

We noted earlier that there is an *inclusio* formed by the words at the end of verses 3 and 34:

> *His kingdom is an everlasting kingdom, and his sovereignty is from generation to generation.* (v. 3)
>
> *For his sovereignty is an everlasting sovereignty, and his kingdom endures from generation to generation.* (v. 34)

The eternal dimension of God and God's kingdom/sovereignty, which so obviously distinguishes the divine from the human, is emphasized by the repetition in Aramaic of the word for 'everlasting' ('forever' and 'everlasting' in the NRSV). The same concept is also conveyed by the expression 'from generation to generation'. This moves a step further than what is stated in the 'refrain' in 4:17, 25 and 32, that 'the Most High has sovereignty over the kingdom of mortals and gives it to whom he will'. Not only is God's sovereignty greater than human sovereignty in that it extends over 'the kingdom of mortals', but it is of a different order because it is everlasting.

A God who does whatever God wants!

Verse 35 appears to state that this most sovereign of all beings does whatever that divine being wants! Well, in a sense this is absolutely correct, although presumably God is constrained by the kind of being God is—which is to say that God acts in a godly way and that is precisely what God 'wants', anyway. I don't think the verse is saying that 'the inhabitants of the earth' are not valuable in God's sight, but rather that God's ways are inscrutable and there is nothing that people can do to make God act in a certain way. The theme here again is the sovereignty of God. No matter how powerful a human being or regime may appear to be, that power is limited in scope compared to God's, and limited in time. Eventually, such power will cease, but God's power will never cease. This may provide some comfort for the powerless in our world who feel oppressed by powers over which they have no control. In the end, such powers are limited and will be held to account by God, the only being with unlimited power in terms both of its scope and its duration.

REFLECTION

An important aspect of any Christian response to God is an acknowledgment of our creatureliness before the all-powerful Creator: we, like Nebuchadnezzar, need to glance heavenward and acknowledge the ultimate sovereignty of God.

NEBUCHADNEZZAR'S RESTORATION

There are similarities between the conclusion to this story and the end of the book of Job: having lost everything, in the end Nebuchadnezzar, like Job, has everything he previously possessed restored to him—and more. Significantly, however, this is not the very end of the story in this chapter. The story ends as it began, with Nebuchadnezzar praising Daniel's God. Thus, the whole story is surrounded by praise of the Most High God (4:2), the King of heaven (v. 37). Indeed, the praises at the beginning and end of the chapter read as though they are in the present, with everything in between as a kind of flashback to the incident that led Nebuchadnezzar to this somewhat surprising position.

My reason returned to me

'My reason returned to me' (v. 36) picks up word for word from 4:34. The phrase is therefore emphasized. However, 'reason' (in the NRSV) may not be the best translation: this is based on the presumption that Nebuchadnezzar lost his reason when 'he was driven away from human society' and 'ate grass like oxen' (4:33). The noun comes from the Aramaic for 'knowing' and occurs elsewhere in Daniel in 2:21 and 5:12.

The verb 'to know' occurs often in chapter 4, most notably in the 'refrain', which NRSV translates thus: 'in order that all who live may *know* that the Most High is sovereign' (4:17). This means that here and in 4:34 and 35, the text specifically picks up on this refrain and shows that Nebuchadnezzar does now 'know' (or has 'learned', to use the NRSV's word in 4:25, 32) both that Daniel's God is sovereign and that he gives sovereignty to whom he will. This sets the restoration of Nebuchadnezzar's kingdom in the right context.

Still more greatness

It may seem strange that the now humbled Nebuchadnezzar has his kingdom returned (in words that recall his boasting in 4:30) and even more greatness added to him (in words that pick up on 4:22). Similar words appear in chapter 2, however, when Daniel explains to the king the significance of the statue in his dream: 'You, O king, the king of kings—to whom the God of heaven has given the kingdom, the power, the might, and the glory... are the head of gold' (2:37–38). They appear again in chapter 5, where Daniel says to Belshazzar, 'O king, the Most High God gave your father Nebuchadnezzar kingship, greatness, glory, and majesty' (5:18). The point is that it is God who gave these things to Nebuchadnezzar, and at last the king acknowledges it.

Praise to the king of heaven

The king's acknowledgment of the source of his greatness and sovereignty was explicit in 4:34 and 35. This is now the third time that Nebuchadnezzar acknowledges characteristics of Daniel's God appropriate to the events that precede the acknowledgment. In chapter 2, Daniel's God is the one who reveals to Nebuchadnezzar through Daniel the meaning of his dream, and the king states, 'Truly, your God is God of gods and Lord of kings and *a revealer of mysteries*' (2:47). In chapter 3, he acknowledges the answer to his own rhetorical question, 'Who is the god that will deliver you out of my hands?' (3:15) when Shadrach, Meshach and Abednego walk out of his furnace unscathed: he says, 'Blessed be the God of Shadrach, Meshach, and Abednego, who has sent his angel and *delivered his servants* who trusted in him... for there is no other god who is *able to deliver* in this way' (3:28–29). Now in chapter 4 he acknowledges that the God who took from the mighty Nebuchadnezzar his kingdom for seven years, then restored it to him again, 'is able to bring low those who walk in pride' (v. 37).

The refrain captures the purpose of chapter 4: 'that all who live may know that the Most High is sovereign over the kingdom of mortals; he gives it to whom he will'. There is nothing implicitly wrong with human power and 'greatness'. There always will be people who hold the reins of considerable power, and some of them will use this power to good effect. It is wrong, however, when such power is held arrogantly, without the acknowledgment that it is not ultimate power: ultimate power and the final decision about where human power resides lie solely in the hands of God.

REFLECTION

How do you view those people or organizations in our world who wield considerable power? Try to think of examples of power well used and examples of the abuse of power, where people seem to usurp the authority that ought to reside solely with God.

27   DANIEL 5:1–4

BELSHAZZAR'S PROFANITY

Chapter 5 starts very abruptly. All the earlier chapters have to do with King Nebuchadnezzar, but here, with no introduction or indication of time, we meet a different king: Belshazzar. It becomes clear as the chapter proceeds that Belshazzar is being portrayed as Nebuchadnezzar's son, but no explanation is given for the jump from one king to the next. Historically it seems that Belshazzar was the son of Nabonidus (four kings later than Nebuchadnezzar and the last of the Babylonian kings), not of Nebuchadnezzar (whose son and successor was Amel-marduk, called Evil-merodach in 2 Kings 25:27). It also seems that Belshazzar was never actually king, although he may have ruled in place of his father when Nabonidus was away from Babylon. Various explanations are offered for these discrepancies, but it may be that historical precision has been sacrificed for the literary effect of drawing together the two kings in order to highlight the differences between them. We might recall the chiastic structure to chapters 2—7, which indicates that the story about Nebuchadnezzar being humbled and the story about Belshazzar being humbled are brought together at the centre of the pattern. The significance of this will become apparent as we proceed through chapter 5.

Ostentatious opulence

Seow says of these verses, 'The opening scene is one of ostentatious opulence' (p. 78). This is indicated by the very first thing said—'King Belshazzar made a great festival'—and emphasized by the repetition of the 'thousand' (v. 1) of his lords who attended, the drinking of wine ('drinking wine' is mentioned twice, but 'wine' appears three times in total and 'drinking' four times) and the three references to gold and silver.

Desecration of the temple vessels

It is not the opulence, however, that is the primary focus of this section. The focus is rather on the misuse of the temple vessels that Nebuchadnezzar had removed from the temple in Jerusalem. This is apparent from further repetition in verses 2 and 3, of a kind we have seen in earlier chapters.

At first glance it may appear that Belshazzar issues his command in verse 2, which is then fulfilled exactly in verse 3. This is true, but the emphasis shifts because of what is left out and what is added in verse 3. Verse 2 draws attention to the fact that the vessels were taken by Nebuchadnezzar; verse 3 omits this reference and focuses instead on the significance of the place where the vessels came from: the house of God in Jerusalem. What this means is that Belshazzar was quite specifically and deliberately misusing Jewish holy objects for his great party, and, moreover, using them in order to praise other gods.

It was bad enough that they had been removed from the temple, but then, that is just what a conquering king would do in those days. There is no indication that Nebuchadnezzar showed the contempt for the vessels that Belshazzar did by using them for his own partying. So what did Belshazzar hope to achieve? Perhaps he wanted to demonstrate that he was greater than Nebuchadnezzar because he could use his father's precious booty in any way he wanted. Perhaps it was actually a direct challenge to the God of the Jews, to show that he, Belshazzar, had no fear of such a God. Or perhaps it was a simple disregard for all things 'holy' as he showed off in front of 'his lords, his wives, and his concubines' (vv. 2–3).

REFLECTION

I think there is considerable ignorance in our society and even within our churches of what holiness means. Can you think of ways our society might be guilty of disregarding things that ought to be set aside for religious use—or even ways that Christians might sometimes be guilty of this also?

The WRITING *on the* WALL

Dreams or visions have been the primary means by which God has spoken to people so far in the book of Daniel, and, indeed, this is true also in the rest of the book. The incident described here is rather different: a human hand appears and writes a message from God on the wall. We are told that 'the king was watching the hand as it wrote' (v. 5), but whether anyone else saw the hand is not clear. It might seem that other people were able to see the writing, because the king offers a reward to 'whoever can read this writing' (v. 7). However, the fact that no one apart from Daniel could even read the writing, let alone interpret it, might imply that this, too, was a vision of some sort, and that nobody else could even see the writing—unless, of course, enabled to do so by God.

An immediate response

In chapter 4 Nebuchadnezzar's pride sparked off an immediate response from God: 'Immediately the sentence was fulfilled against Nebuchadnezzar' (4:33). The same occurs in chapter 5, where it is now Belshazzar's pride and his desecration of the temple vessels that provoke an immediate response from God: 'Immediately the fingers of a human hand appeared' (v. 5). The comparison between these two kings, and the way God responds to their pride and they respond to God's response, continues.

The king's terror

Very similar words to verse 6 are found in chapter 7, where Daniel describes his distress after the visions he has seen: 'As for me, Daniel, my thoughts greatly terrified me, and my face turned pale' (7:28). In 4:19, Daniel was distressed and King Nebuchadnezzar told him not to be afraid (although the king himself had earlier been terrified by his visions). Here in chapter 5, it is King Belshazzar whose terror is described, emphasized by repetition in verses 6 and 9: 'Then the king's face turned pale, and his thoughts terrified him. His limbs gave way, and his knees knocked together… Then King Belshazzar became greatly terrified and his face turned pale.' The expression 'his limbs gave way' is literally 'the knots of his hips loosened', which might imply that his legs gave way (though his knees wouldn't then have knocked!), or may mean that he lost control of his bowels. Either way, the picture is of someone who is unhinged by fear. This is further emphasized by the next few words, 'The king cried aloud' (v. 7). They stand in contrast to Nebuchadnezzar in the previous chapter who, despite his own fear, managed to maintain control and even offer words of comfort to Daniel.

Having previously shown a patent disregard for holy things, Belshazzar is now faced with a direct communication from the holy God of the Jews—and he is terrified! The Hebrew word for 'fear' (the Aramaic is similar) is like the English word: it can portray terror of something or an appropriate reverence. An encounter with God may be 'fearful' in either or both of these ways. For someone like Belshazzar, who has been contemptuous of holy things, it may well be a terrifying experience.

The Babylonian wise men

Just as in chapters 2 and 4, the Babylonian wise men are called upon first to give the interpretation (v. 7). Whatever King Belshazzar may have expected, the reader knows by now that they will be unable to provide the interpretation. It is a bit of a puzzle, though, that the wise men are unable even to read the writing (v. 8). It may be, as I suggested above, that the hand and the writing were a vision that only King Belshazzar could see. In this case, rather like in chapter 2, the wise men would have to tell King Belshazzar what he had seen *and* interpret it for him. However, there is no clear indication in the text that they could not even see the writing, so it may be that the words were in 'unpointed' Aramaic: consonants without any vowels supplied, which could therefore have been read in various different ways.

REFLECTION

The phrase 'writing on the wall' has become a stock phrase in English, even if people don't know that it comes from Daniel. What might be the 'writing on the wall' for us (or our country) at this time?

LET DANIEL BE CALLED

Most of the rest of this chapter takes the form of three speeches: one by the queen, one by King Belshazzar and a long speech by Daniel. This section is the queen's speech, but just who is 'the queen'?

The queen

We read in 5:2 that Belshazzar's wives (and concubines) were with him at his great festival, so the queen who 'came into the banqueting hall' (v. 10) is likely to be someone else. Besides, the king's wives are unlikely to have dared to approach him unbidden, which, it seems, constituted an offence punishable by death (see Esther 4:11). 'The queen' here is probably someone with more authority than the king's wives, and the person who best fits this picture and might also take the title 'queen' is the queen mother. In the context of this story, most scholars conclude that the person in question is Nebuchad-nezzar's wife, a woman named Nitocris who had a reputation as a wise and powerful queen. Her references to 'your father' (v. 11) would fit with this conclusion, as would her knowledge of Daniel's interaction with Nebuchadnezzar. The fact that it is the queen mother who takes the initiative here, not Belshazzar, heightens the contrast between the two kings. The fact that this 'queen' is probably intended to be Nebuchadnezzar's wife also adds a touch of irony, because in a way the former king is continuing to exert his influence, while his weak 'son', who presumed to deride the holy God, proves unable to act for himself.

Daniel's credentials

The expression 'endowed with a spirit of the holy gods', used to describe Daniel, occurs in chapter 4 in the mouth of Nebuchad-nezzar, and twice in chapter 5, once here in the queen's speech (v. 11) and once when Belshazzar speaks. Again it serves to link the two chapters and to hark back to Nebuchadnezzar. With regard to the significance of the other words used to describe Daniel, I cannot do better here than to quote Goldingay:

The skills attributed to Daniel (vv. 11—12) relate directly to the interpretation of a portent... 'Insight' ['enlightenment' in the NRSV]... suggests illumination from God, the source of light (2:22). 'Ability' ['understanding']... indicates that Daniel not only possesses intellect or talent; he knows how to use it, by God's gift (according to 1:17). 'Wisdom' ... denotes in Daniel the supernatural intuition of an interpreter of dreams or omens, that wisdom which also belongs supremely to God (2:20) and which as his gift makes Daniel outstanding among sages (1:17; 2:21, 23). 'Knowledge'... likewise denotes the God-given supernatural knowledge of an interpreter (1:17; 2:21). The reference to 'the spirit of the holy deity'/ 'a remarkable spirit' (4:8) underlines the implication that Daniel's extraordinary ability comes from God. The outworking of his gifts develops these points. (pp. 109—10)

The description of Daniel here draws on descriptions earlier in the book to emphasize that, able as he may be, what really counts in this context is that he is enabled or empowered by God.

Loosening knots

The expression 'solve problems' (v. 12; also 5:16) is literally 'loosen knots'. There is a play on words here which isn't apparent in English translations: as we noted previously, the phrase translated 'his limbs gave way', referring to Belshazzar in 5:6, is literally 'the knots of his hips loosened'. Thus, while in the earlier verse 'loosening knots' refers to Belshazzar's lack of control, here and in 5:16 it anticipates Daniel's God-given control over the situation.

Earlier in the chapter, Belshazzar is portrayed as a powerful ruler who shows complete disregard for the God of the Jews. In this section, Daniel is portrayed as a man whose 'power' comes from God. We already know from earlier in the book, and are reminded by these words, that he is a man who holds his God in very high regard. Daniel's 'power' may not seem very dramatic compared to Belshazzar's, but the powerful king has lost control while this passage hints that Daniel's powers will enable him to take control of the situation.

REFLECTION

In what ways does God's empowering enable Christians to stay in control when things go wrong?

DANIEL'S REPUTATION PRECEDES HIM

This section consists of Belshazzar's words, and it is significant that he really has little new to say: almost everything he says here has been said before in this chapter, as can be clearly seen by comparing verses 13–16 with verses 11, 8, 12 and 7 in that order.

Daniel, one of the exiles

There is one thing that the king says, though, which does not appear earlier in the chapter: his first words, 'So you are Daniel, one of the exiles of Judah, whom my father the king brought from Judah?' (v. 13). These words emphasize that Daniel is a foreigner, that he is a captive and, moveover, that he was brought into exile by Belshazzar's own father. Of course, the reader now knows all these things, so it may be that the storyteller is including these words to help develop Belshazzar's character. Thus, the only new thing that King Belshazzar has to say emphasizes Daniel's inferiority. This fits with the picture developing of an arrogant, power-hungry but perhaps decidedly in-secure king. There is also a notable omission from Belshazzar's words in verse 14: on the four other occasions when the expression appears, it is 'a spirit of the holy gods', but here it is just 'a spirit of the gods'. This may be a further subtle indication of Belshazzar's disregard for all things holy, which was portrayed so clearly earlier in the chapter. The same may be true about the change from 'wisdom like the wisdom of the gods' to 'excellent wisdom' (v. 14).

I have heard that you...

Corresponding to the picture of Belshazzar as described above is his seemingly reluctant admission of Daniel's 'credentials'. He seems not to know these things first-hand, and only repeats what the queen told him earlier. Moreover, the repeated 'I have heard of you' (or 'I have heard that you') may imply a degree of scepticism: 'people say that you're all these things—now prove it!' The change from (literally) 'anyone who reads the writing and tells me its interpretation' to 'if you are able to read the writing and tell me its interpretation' may again be intended to cast doubt on Daniel's abilities.

Interpretation

'Interpretation' is an important word in chapters 2, 4 and 5 (it is used thirteen times in chapter 2, eight times in chapter 4 and eleven times in this chapter). This section of chapter 5 is anticipated by the words at the end of the previous one, where the queen says, 'Now let Daniel be called, and he will give the interpretation' (5:12). The word 'interpretation' then occurs five times in these four verses. The concept of 'interpretation' is a key one throughout the book of Daniel: in the first half of the book, only Daniel has the ability to interpret what it is that God is saying. The sovereign, holy God is speaking and it needs someone empowered by him to interpret those words. It looks as though Belshazzar has to acknowledge reluctantly that this is the case: he therefore has to humble himself and accept the help of this foreign exile. As we shall see later, God continues to speak in the second half of the book, but interpretation becomes more complicated.

REFLECTION

Daniel's reputation goes before him. It rather looks as though Daniel is about the last person King Belshazzar would have wanted to consult, but in times of dire need he is forced to turn to this foreign exile. Having the right kind of reputation is very important. If we are known as people who hear and interpret 'the word of God', it may well be (and it has been in my experience) that other people come to us in time of dire need—and sometimes they may include people who seem to be very sceptical even about the existence of God.

DANIEL *the* PROPHET

In the previous two sections we have had two short speeches: first the queen's speech in which she advises, 'Let Daniel be called', then King Belshazzar's speech in which he reluctantly consults Daniel. The next three sections contain Daniel's speech, which falls into three parts. First, Daniel harks back to Nebuchadnezzar's humbling. Second, he turns this back on Belshazzar, explaining how he has not humbled himself. Finally, Daniel gives the interpretation of the words that Belshazzar saw written on the wall. This means, of course, that the interpretation that Belshazzar seeks is held to the very end—so we can imagine his impatience building.

Prophecy at its best

Lucas notes, 'Many have compared Daniel's speech to those of the Hebrew prophets who confronted the kings of Israel and Judah' (p. 132). In our Old Testament, Daniel is included as one of the four 'major' prophets: Isaiah, Jeremiah, Ezekiel and Daniel. In fact, however, Daniel is a very different kind of book from Isaiah, Jeremiah and Ezekiel (although the minor prophets are much more diverse). It contains little that would encourage us to consider it as the same kind of material, but Daniel's words to Belshazzar here may give some grounds for doing so: an individual courageously declares to the king the words that he believes God would have him say, including a severe indictment of the way the king has acted. This is a good example of Old Testament prophecy at its best—bringing God's perspective to bear on contemporary events in a clear and courageous way.

Let your gifts be for yourself

Commentators have puzzled over Daniel's words, 'Let your gifts be for yourself, or give your rewards to someone else!' (v. 17). These words are hardly going to endear him to the king, and seem rather like a slap in the face—a dangerous thing to give to so powerful a figure. Moreover, Daniel had been courteous in his dealings with Nebuchadnezzar. He had also, in the past, accepted the rewards offered—and will eventually do so in this instance, too. Lederach is probably right when he suggests these reasons for Daniel's rejection of Belshazzar's gifts: 'First, he does not want to be under obligation to Belshazzar. Second, he does not want the interpretation to appear connected with personal profit. Third, Daniel uses God's gifts for God's glory rather than for personal advantage' (p. 115).

It seems that there is nothing wrong with accepting the 'payment' offered for the service he renders; what is of concern is the giver's motive for offering such payment and possible motives for accepting payment. There are similarities here to the 'stipend' paid to vicars and some pastors and other ministers: they are not paid for what they do, but given a 'living' to enable them to undertake the task God calls them to. At its best, this means that the church doesn't pay such leaders to do what it wants them to, but frees them to do what God wants them to, even if at times the church doesn't much like it.

Telling Nebuchadnezzar's story

Daniel starts off by telling the story about Nebuchadnezzar related in chapter 4 (in words very similar to those used twice in that chapter). In this way he draws on past events that Belshazzar must have known about, and interprets them in relation to the king's own circumstances. Moreover, this picks up on what was probably intended as a slight by Belshazzar: 'So you are Daniel, one of the exiles of Judah, whom my father the king brought from Judah?' (5:13). Belshazzar may be intending to say, 'You are only an exile captured by my father'; Daniel effectively replies, 'Yes, but great as your father was, he was humbled by my God.' Daniel builds up this account to a climax, which consists of the words of the refrain from 4:17, 25, 32: 'until he learned that the Most High God has sovereignty over the kingdom of mortals, and sets over it whomsoever he will' (v. 21). From a literary perspective, the contrast between the two kings is thus drawn even more sharply.

REFLECTION

Old Testament prophecy is less about predicting the future (though it does contain some of this), and more about bringing God's perspective (often in judgment) on society and sometimes upon individuals. What might be the place of such prophecy today?

LIKE FATHER, LIKE SON, *but* WORSE!

In the previous section, Daniel reiterated the story of Nebuchadnezzar's fall due to his pride. It was pretty obvious what he was building up to, but now he makes it explicit: even though God dealt with his father's arrogance in this way, still Belshazzar, the son, has not learned the lesson and has 'not humbled his heart' (v. 22). This is where the focus of chapter 5 lies. Again, it is not really about Daniel himself; rather, he functions as God's representative in a battle between 'the Lord of heaven' and the most powerful ruler on earth (although not for much longer!). This ties in with a key question in the book of Daniel: who is really in control of events, the seemingly powerful kings of human kingdoms, or the God of the Jews who reigns in heaven? Four accusations are levelled at King Belshazzar, all of which are connected to this question.

You have not humbled your heart

The previous section ended with the refrain from chapter 4: 'until he learned that the Most High God has sovereignty over the kingdom of mortals, and sets over it whomsoever he will'. Eventually Nebuchadnezzar had learned this lesson. Belshazzar, it seems, never has. His lack of humility is expressed twice, in opposite ways: 'you... have not humbled your heart' (v. 22) and 'you have exalted yourself against the Lord of heaven' (v. 23a). His is the sin of pride, and one of the ways in which this pride is displayed is through his misuse of the temple vessels.

Desecration of the temple vessels

We considered the desecration of the vessels earlier in the chapter: whatever were Belshazzar's precise motives for taking them and using them for profane purposes, by his action he showed a patent disregard for things set aside for God, and demonstrated that he saw himself as above the religious restrictions that others observed. He was effectively exalting himself over the God of the Jews.

Praising gods who are no gods at all

Belshazzar didn't just use the temple vessels for feasting, however. He used these items from the temple of the God of the Jews to worship other gods. Daniel makes the point here that these gods 'do not see or hear or know' (v. 23): they are lifeless objects with no power of their own. This is a theme that appears elsewhere in the Old Testament. For example, in Deuteronomy 4:28 the exile in Babylon, which is the background to the book of Daniel, is anticipated, and the writer says, 'There you will serve other gods made by human hands, objects of wood and stone that neither see, nor hear, nor eat, nor smell.'

Not honouring the true God

By contrast, Belshazzar has not given honour to the one God who is real, the God 'in whose power is your very breath, and to whom belong all your ways' (v. 23b). This is where the contrast between Nebuchadnezzar and Belshazzar is drawn most sharply. At the height of his pride Nebuchadnezzar had said, 'Is this not magnificent Babylon, which I have built as a royal capital by my mighty power and for my glorious majesty' (4:30), and here 'majesty' is the same word as 'honoured' in 5:23. But later he saw things differently, lifted his eyes to heaven and 'blessed the Most High, and praised and honoured the one who lives for ever' (4:34). As a result of his humility, he had his 'majesty' (same word as 'honour') restored (4:36), but he still said, 'Now I, Nebuchadnezzar, praise and extol and honour the King of heaven, for all his works are truth, and his ways are justice; and he is able to bring low those who walk in pride' (4:37). With these words chapter 4 ended, and with the words in 5:23, 'but the God in whose power is your very breath, and to whom belong all your ways, you have not honoured', the essence of the difference between the two kings, Nebuchadnezzar and Belshazzar, is established.

REFLECTION

Humility before God is a key aspect of Old Testament faith and of Christian faith today. Whatever our theology, it is important to acknowledge our limitations, and to accept that ultimately sovereignty rests only with God.

INTERPRETING *for* BELSHAZZAR

At last, Daniel gets to the interpretation for which Belshazzar has been waiting. It may be that Daniel deliberately held back the interpretation to the end, knowing that he had a 'captive audience' (ironically, as Belshazzar was keen to point out that Daniel was a captive of the Babylonian empire—captured, moreover, by Belshazzar's father). This enabled him to preach his prophetic sermon to Belshazzar first. Thus, typical of Daniel, he uses the occasion well to say to Belshazzar what he needs to hear. Moreover, Daniel's words have established the context within which the interpretation will fit. The judgment pronounced on the king will make sense against this background. Alternatively (or perhaps in addition), the narrator may be building up the suspense before reaching the climax of the chapter: not only is Belshazzar kept waiting for the interpretation, but so too is the reader. We noted earlier that 'interpretation' is an important theme in this chapter. The word occurs often and builds up our expectations concerning the interpretation, which we know by now that Daniel will be able to provide. But we too, like the king, have first to hear reiterated the story of Nebuchadnezzar's pride, fresh in our minds from the previous chapter, and then read about Belshazzar's pride. This helps to impress upon us a key theme that runs through both chapters 4 and 5: human pride standing in the way of God's sovereignty. The interpretation is given in light of this theme.

The interpretation

The writing itself, '*mene, mene, tekel* and *parsin*' appears to be a list of terms for different coins: *mene* = mina; *tekel* = shekel; *parsin* = halves (of shekels or minas?). It is possible that the first *mene* is the verb 'numbered', so that we get 'numbered as a mina, a shekel, and halves'. But when Daniel interprets the words, he renders them all with verbs: *mene* = numbered; *tekel* = weighed; *parsin* = divided. It may be that there is a play on words, such that Daniel is linking a similar verb to each of the nouns; there is probably also a play between *parsin* and 'Persian', the kingdom that would conquer the Babylonians.

It may also be that the writing on the wall consisted simply of a continuous string of consonants without any vowels added: *mn'tqlprs*. This might explain why the Babylonian wise men were unable to read it (although I suggested above that they may not even have been able to see it). It would also allow Daniel to read the words both as a string of nouns and as a string of verbs, which would take different vowels. Certainly it is an example of Daniel's ability, with the help of God, to 'explain riddles and solve problems' (literally 'loosen knots'; see 5:12).

The message

The message for Belshazzar is very clear, and it falls into three parts. First, Belshazzar's days are numbered and are to be brought to an end (past tense in Aramaic because God has already set it in motion). This is a key theme in the book of Daniel: even when a foreign ruler seems to be controlling the lives of the Jews, his times are in God's hands, and God will ensure that if he oversteps the mark set by God, his reign will be brought to an end. Second, Belshazzar has been 'weighed'. God has not ignored what the king has done, but rather has taken it into account and will mete out the appropriate judgment. Third, that judgment is about to be actioned: Belshazzar's kingdom is soon to fall and be divided among the Medes and the Persians.

These three points continue to have relevance today. First, as the psalmist says, 'My times are in your hand' (Psalm 31:15). Ultimately, God does oversee our 'times' and 'numbers' our days, not in the sense of setting precise limits, but by establishing appropriate boundaries. Second, our actions do matter to God: it is not that we 'earn our salvation', but God does expect us to act in certain ways and holds us accountable for what we do. Third, God is a God of justice and of judgment. We may not always see the outworking of this in our own lives and experience, but the Bible assures us that the Lord is a God of justice.

REFLECTION

Do these three points correlate with your experience?
What questions do they raise for you?

BELSHAZZAR KILLED

The speeches by the queen, Belshazzar and Daniel are over and the chapter now comes to a very quick conclusion. There are two parts to this conclusion: first, Daniel receives what he deserves, the rewards promised by Belshazzar (although initially Daniel had refused them); then Belshazzar receives what he deserves. He is killed by the army of Darius the Mede.

Daniel's reward

In verse 29, Daniel is rewarded exactly as was promised earlier, first to the Babylonian wise men (5:7) and then to Daniel himself (5:16). It is not clear whether 'third' actually means of third highest authority after Belshazzar and one other person (some suggest the queen mother), or whether 'third' is the title of an office. Either way, though, Daniel, the Jewish exile, is given a very high rank in the Babylonian court. Here again Daniel is like Joseph to whom, after he had interpreted his dream, Pharaoh said, 'You shall be over my house, and all my people shall order themselves as you command; only with regard to the throne will I be greater than you.' Pharaoh then placed his own signet ring on Joseph's hand, put on him a garment of fine linen and placed a gold chain round his neck (see Genesis 41:38–45). In both cases the Israelite/Jew remains faithful to his God even under great pressure and with vigorous opposition; in both cases his faithfulness is rewarded and his God-given abilities lead him to high office within a foreign court.

Darius the Mede

We encounter a problem with Darius the Mede (v. 31): there is no record anywhere else of a king called Darius the Mede (although there are Persian kings called Darius), and Babylon fell not to Median forces but to the Persians under King Cyrus. There are three main positions held by scholars:

• The majority argue that 'Darius the Mede' is a literary construct rather than a historical person, based on texts that may mention a Median conquest of Babylon (Isaiah 13:17; 21:2; Jeremiah 51:11, 28).

- Some scholars hold that 'Darius the Mede' is another name for the general Gobryas (or Gubaru or Ugbaru, all apparently variations of the same name), who led the actual capture of Babylon on behalf of Cyrus, and may have governed Babylon in the first instance. There is no evidence that this general was ever called Darius, however.

- It has been argued that 'Darius the Mede' is another name for Cyrus, based on the possible translation of 6:28, 'Daniel prospered in the reign of Darius, that is, the reign of Cyrus the Persian.' As Lucas explains, 'Since Cyrus took over the Median empire and had a Median mother, he could be called a Mede, even "king of the Medes." Moreover, he would have been about sixty-two when he conquered Babylon' (p. 136). As Lucas continues, however, 'The statement that Darius' father was Ahasuerus (Daniel 9:1) remains problematic, since Cyrus' father was named Cambyses'. Also, this is not the most obvious translation of the Aramaic text.

In the end, with the information currently available to us, the identity of Darius the Mede remains problematic, and it is possible that more than one historical person lies behind the biblical character. Nonetheless, he represents the immediate fulfilment of God's words to Belshazzar in the writing on the wall.

By contrast to the previous chapter, events in chapter 5 move very quickly: from start to finish it all takes place in one night. Belshazzar's actions that evening demonstrate clearly his arrogant disregard for holy things and for the God of the Jews, so God, through Daniel, tells him that he has been found wanting, and that hence the days of his kingdom are numbered and it will be divided between the Medes and the Persians. That very night the words are fulfilled through 'Darius the Mede'. The book of Daniel portrays a God who is in control of world events. Sometimes that control is demonstrated immediately, but sometimes events take much longer and in the meantime the people of God (and others) may suffer severely.

REFLECTION

How do you cope when at times God seems to act instantly, while at other times God seems to act very slowly, if at all, and innocent people suffer in the meantime?

DANIEL DISTINGUISHES HIMSELF

There are two significant elements of structure and style which should be noted in relation to this chapter. Firstly, we recall that chapters 2—7 are organized chiastically, so that this chapter is paired with chapter 3 (see Introduction, p. 17). Indeed, although there are notable differences between chapters 3 and 6, they do seem deliberately to parallel each other, as Lucas explains (p. 145):

> In both stories, jealous colleagues accuse the Jews of slighting the king's authority and insist that the king carry out the death sentence he has decreed. He does so, ensuring as best he can that there is no way that they can escape. There is mention of the possibility that God might deliver them. He does so by sending one of his messengers to the place of execution to keep the Jews unharmed. The king then orders their release and the subjection of those who accused them to the same form of death. The king declares that all peoples are to recognize the unique power of the God whom the Jews worship. The stories end by noting how the Jews continue to flourish.

As in chapters 4 and 5, however, one of the starkest contrasts is between the responses of the two kings. Here Darius is portrayed in a much more positive light than is Nebuchadnezzar in chapter 3.

Secondly, this chapter itself seems to be structured chiastically—as, indeed, is chapter 3:

A Introduction: Daniel's success (6:1–3)
  B Darius signs an injunction but Daniel takes his stand (6:4–10)
    C Daniel's colleagues plan his death (6:11–15)
      D Darius hopes for Daniel's deliverance (6:16–18)
      D Darius witnesses Daniel's deliverance (6:19–23)
    C Daniel's colleagues meet with their death (6:24)
  B Darius signs an edict and takes his stand (6:25–27)
A Conclusion: Daniel's success (6:28)

Thus the chapter starts and finishes with Daniel's 'success' and revolves around his deliverance at its centre.

King Darius

The king pictured in this story may be Darius I Hystaspis (522–486BC), who is renowned for his organization of the Persian kingdom into satrapies. (In verse 1, it appears that Darius sets three men over the whole kingdom, and under them 120 governors, or satraps, of the various regions, or satrapies, of the kingdom.) This identification doesn't correlate with the 'Darius the Mede' pictured in the previous chapter, who conquered the Babylonian kingdom ruled by King Belshazzar. As noted earlier, the king of Babylon at the time of its fall was Nabonidus, and the conquering king was Cyrus of Persia. Longman argues that it is likely that 'Darius is a throne name for someone ruling in Babylon at the behest of Cyrus' (p. 157). Personally, I am happier to live with uncertainty, in light of the fact that the Darius pictured in Daniel does not fit well with what we know of the history of the time. Whoever the king is, he is very well disposed towards Daniel, but comes across as a rather weak character, especially by contrast with Daniel himself.

Daniel's progression

Daniel progresses from being a mere slave to becoming one of the wisest men in the kingdom (in ch. 1). He then becomes the head of the wise men (ch. 2) before being consulted as King Nebuchadnezzar's personal adviser (ch. 4). Later he is promoted to 'third' in Belshazzar's kingdom (ch. 5); and now King Darius intends 'to appoint him over the whole kingdom' (v. 3). This foreign man has distinguished himself above all the other rulers, and, try as they might, they fail to find any fault in him (hence the four times repeated reference to their attempt to 'find grounds for complaint' against Daniel in verses 4 and 5). Here indeed is an example of a faithful believer performing exceedingly well in high office, and winning both respect and hatred as a result.

Daniel is a faithful believer who holds very high office and excels at his job. Like many in high office, however—perhaps especially those known to have a strong belief in God—Daniel had people watching his every move to try to bring him down. He proved faultless, but many in high office make mistakes, sometimes very public mistakes.

REFLECTION

Christians in position of leadership need our support even when they prove not to be as exemplary as Daniel.

36   DANIEL 6:6–9

The SCHEME *against* DANIEL

In the previous section we saw that Daniel distinguished himself, both in terms of his conduct in his high office within King Darius' government, and also implicitly in his religious conduct. The other rulers in Darius' government come across in a bad light. Indeed, they focus on Daniel's exemplary religious conduct in order, so they think, to bring him down. King Darius is not cast in a particularly good light either. The only one who really comes out of this well is Daniel.

Like headless chickens!

The other rulers appear as one group of people, 'the presidents and satraps' (6:3, 4, 6), who all (122 of them!) move around together in a throng. First, we learned that Daniel distinguished himself over 'all the other presidents and satraps' (6:3); next we were told that 'the presidents and the satraps tried to find grounds for complaint against Daniel' (6:4); now it is stated that 'the presidents and satraps conspired and came to the king' (v. 6). 'Conspired and came' is one word in Aramaic, and is used to characterize these men the next two times we encounter them: they are called 'the conspirators' in 6:11 and 15, using the same Aramaic word as here. The word appears to mean 'to be in a throng' or 'to make a tumult', with overtones here of conspiracy. Moreover, they resort to lying in order to persuade the king to do what they want. They state that 'all the presidents of the kingdom... are agreed that the king should establish an ordinance' (v. 7)—but, of course, the king's favoured president is not among this group. The picture is of all 122 men scurrying round like the proverbial headless chickens, trying desperately to find a way to bring Daniel down. The final time we encounter these men is in 6:24, where they are described as 'those who had accused Daniel' (literally, 'those who ate pieces of Daniel'). There, all 122 of them plus their families are thrown in a group to the lions: they go to their end in a throng just as they did everything else in a throng.

It is a sad truth that people often do seek ways to bring Christians down, especially those Christians who hold positions of responsibility and those who are prepared to stand out from the crowd because of their beliefs. Here, the crowd is portrayed like a flock of sheep who follow one another around, bleating about Daniel. Standing out from the crowd is not easy, particularly when it turns against you. Can you think of ways in which you should stand out from the crowd, even if it risks the crowd turning on you?

A question of worship

These men had discovered that they could not fault Daniel in the performance of his duties. They also knew that he was exemplary in his faithfulness to his God, so they devised a trap whereby he would be forced to choose between worshipping his God and worshipping King Darius. Presumably Daniel could have chosen to continue his worship in secret for the thirty-day period, but he knew that this would mean following the law of the Medes and the Persians rather than God's law, and would implicitly amount to raising Darius above his own God.

The law of his God

An important theme in this chapter is the contrast between, and the competing demands of, the law of Daniel's God and the law of the Medes and the Persians. There is considerable irony in the repeated affirmation that the law of the Medes and the Persians cannot be revoked: the narratives here and in chapter 3 show that God can revoke any human law, and that only God's law is eternal and beyond being revoked. There are times when the law of the land and God's law come into conflict. At those times, it is God's law that must be the Christian's higher priority—which means that there is a time for Christians to engage in civil disobedience. Can you envisage situations where this might be the case in the future?

PRAYER

Sovereign God, we pray for those who are suffering because they have been brave enough to stand out from the crowd for what they believe, and for those who face the conflict between God's law and the law of the land.

37 DANIEL 6:10–13

DANIEL PRAYS REGARDLESS

The focus shifts in verse 10 from the bustling 'presidents and satraps' on to Daniel, who takes no dramatic action either to defy the king deliberately or to comply with the decree he has issued. Rather, Daniel simply goes about his normal business—which includes praying upon his knees three times a day by a window that is open towards Jerusalem. Of course, this means that he is in view of anyone who cares to watch. Presumably, at least one of the 'presidents and satraps' has seen him praying like this before, and now they are waiting to catch him in order to report to the king that Daniel has breached the recently issued edict.

A man of prayer

So far as we can tell, there was no actual requirement in God's law to pray three times a day (Psalm 55:17 offers the closest parallel, but see the seven times daily prayer in Psalm 119:164), or to pray upon one's knees (standing was the usual position for prayer, although prayer in a kneeling position and prostrate also feature in the Bible), or to pray towards Jerusalem (1 Kings 8:35 provides the clearest example). Rather, Daniel is portrayed here as a man whose regular habit was to pray three times daily, in a humble position on his knees, and facing towards the traditional centre of Jewish worship, Jerusalem. Chapter 9 gives a sample of the kind of prayer Daniel prayed, and it is an excellent example of humble and godly prayer, as we shall see later. Moreover, Daniel wasn't to be deterred from his usual practice of prayer, even under threat of death. Clearly, Daniel is portrayed as a man for whom prayer was so important that it had to continue regardless of the circumstances.

Prayer—seeking God

Two words for 'prayer' occur in this chapter. The word in verse 10 (Daniel got 'down on his knees three times a day to *pray*') occurs only here in Daniel (and only in Ezra 6:10 elsewhere in the Old Testament). A different word occurs in verses 7, 11, 12 and 13. This is a word meaning 'seek', and it is used in that more ordinary sense in 6:4, as well as in 2:13, 16, 18, 23, 49; 4:36 and 7:16. There is a play on this word and the word 'find' in chapter 6. First, 'the presidents and the satraps *sought* to *find* grounds for complaint against Daniel' (and 'they could *find* no grounds of complaint', then confess, 'We shall not *find* any ground for complaint', adding, 'unless we *find* it in connection with the law of his God'). The decree they persuade the king to issue condemns anyone who '*seeks* [or 'petitions'] anyone, divine or human' except the king. They then *find* Daniel *seeking* God and proceed to tell the king that he is '*seeking* three times a day'. Thus the presidents and satraps *seek* to *find* ways to bring Daniel down, and they end up *finding* Daniel *seeking* God. It seems that Daniel's appropriate seeking is contrasted with the seeking of the presidents and satraps.

Prayer is the key theme of this section. Daniel is exemplary in his commitment to pray regardless of the circumstances. He seems to make no great show of his prayer, or to try to hide it, but he continues praying in his usual way even under threat of death. This word for prayer, meaning 'seek', is also significant. Prayer is not about us praising God, or thanking God, or petitioning God; rather it is about 'seeking' God, both seeking relationship with him and also seeking his mind on the matters about which we pray.

'Daniel... pays no attention to you!'

There is a play on words in the presidents' and satraps' statement that 'Daniel... pays no *attention* to you, O king' in verse 13. The same word occurred in 6:2 where the satraps gave *account* to the presidents 'so that the king might suffer no loss'. The word occurs again in 6:26, where Darius says, 'I make *a decree*.' It is difficult to capture the force of this in English, but it shows that the satraps were *accountable* to Daniel and the other presidents at the beginning of the chapter; Daniel refused to be held ultimately *accountable* to King Darius in the middle of the chapter; and at the end of the chapter Darius makes everyone *accountable*, by a law he passes, to 'tremble and fear before the God of Daniel'. Ultimate 'accountability' is owed to God and none other.

REFLECTION

Is prayer sufficiently important for you that you would continue to pray openly even if it might cost you your life? Consider whether there are times when we are too secretive about prayer, and if there are times when we make too much of a show of prayer.

MAY YOUR GOD DELIVER YOU

We noted earlier that chapter 6 is in some ways very similar to chapter 3, and that the chiastic structure of chapters 2—7 brings these two chapters together. We also noted that chapters 3 and 6 are different because of the attitudes of the two kings involved. In this section we see how different the attitude of Darius is from that displayed earlier by Nebuchadnezzar.

The king is distressed

In chapter 2, Nebuchadnezzar's 'spirit was troubled' because of a dream he did not understand (2:1). In chapter 4 he saw a dream that 'frightened' him, and visions that 'terrified' him (4:5). Indeed, in that chapter Daniel too was 'severely distressed' and 'terrified' by the dream (4:19). Here the NRSV tells us that King Darius 'was very much distressed' (v. 14), so much so that 'sleep fled from him' (v. 18). However, his distress is of a very different sort from that displayed earlier by Nebuchadnezzar. Firstly, he is not scared by a dream that he doesn't understand; and secondly, the word used is different and is used only here in Daniel. Indeed, as Goldingay points out, it might better be translated as 'displeased' rather than 'distressed' (p. 121). The precise reason for his great 'distress' or 'displeasure' is not indicated, but it arises from the fact that he has been tricked into condemning to death his most trusted adviser. However the word is translated, Darius reacts very strongly to this treatment of Daniel. This provides quite a contrast with Nebuchadnezzar in chapter 3, where he was in a 'furious rage' with Shadrach, Meshach and Abednego (3:13). Both kings react with great emotion: one reacts with unrighteous anger against faithful believers, while the other reacts with righteous concern for a faithful believer.

The king is determined

In chapter 3 Nebuchadnezzar was determined to destroy the three Jews, and went to great lengths to ensure that it happened, heating the furnace to a great temperature and getting his strongest guards to bind Shadrach, Meshach and Abednego. Here Darius is determined to deliver (or 'save' in NRSV) Daniel from destruction (v. 14), and he too goes to great lengths in order to achieve this end. But his efforts, laudable as they are, prove just as futile as Nebuchadnezzar's much less commendable efforts.

But only God can deliver

In verse 16, we meet the final contrast in this section between the two kings. In 3:15 Nebuchadnezzar issued the following arrogant challenge to Shadrach, Meshach and Abednego (and effectively to their God): 'Who is the god that will deliver you out of my hands?' By contrast, Darius says to Daniel as he is thrown into the den of lions, 'May your God, whom you faithfully serve, deliver you!' This word 'deliver' is the same word that the NRSV translates as 'save' in verse 14. What Darius had tried but failed to do, he now hopes that Daniel's God will do. Of course, we as readers know that God can do it: the word 'deliver' occurs elsewhere in Daniel only in chapter 3, and there we learn that God can deliver those who serve him faithfully. Indeed, Nebuchadnezzar himself stated at the end of the chapter, 'Blessed be the God of Shadrach, Meshach, and Abednego, who has sent his angel and delivered his servants who trusted in him' (3:28). The words of the two kings form something of a pivot around which the two chapters revolve, one expressing his belief that God cannot deliver, the other expressing his hope that God will deliver. The stone 'laid on the mouth of the den' (v. 17) is just like the stone rolled across a tomb: when Darius seals it, he is effectively acknowledging that Daniel is dead and there is nothing he can do about it. While Darius undoubtedly is portrayed in a much better light than Nebuchadnezzar, they both need to learn the same lesson: only God can deliver. It looks as though both of them believed that the power to 'deliver' or 'save' lay in their hands; both needed to learn that in the end 'deliverance' belongs to God and to God alone. The same is true today. Regardless of how 'nice' people seem to be (or how 'nice' they actually are!), the power to 'deliver' or 'save' remains with God and not with people. No one has the power to save themselves or anyone else; rather, people need to turn to God for salvation.

PRAYER

Sovereign God, may we show by our lives our belief that salvation comes from you. Help us to bring others to realize this truth, too.

DANIEL DELIVERED

The king has had a sleepless night worrying about what has happened to Daniel. He had issued the edict which had surely resulted in Daniel's death; he had sealed the stone over the mouth of the den with his own seal (presumably so that any disturbance would be obvious). Now it is morning and he goes to see what has happened. Despite the seeming certainty that Daniel will be dead, Darius still retains some hope.

The king speaks

As Daniel was thrown to the lions, Darius said to him, 'May your God, whom you faithfully serve, deliver you!' (6:16). Now he speaks again to Daniel: 'O Daniel, servant of the living God, has your God whom you faithfully serve been able to deliver you from the lions?' (v. 20). There are two points in particular to note here. First, the elements repeated in verses 16 and 20 draw attention to two things: Daniel's 'faithful service' of his God, and the hope that God will 'deliver' him. The king has clearly been impressed with Daniel's faithfulness to his God, and he maintains hope that this God really is a God of salvation.

Second, Darius refers to Daniel's God as 'the living God'. Only in this chapter is the expression used of God: twice Darius refers to God in this way. However, in 4:34 Nebuchadnezzar says similar words: 'I blessed the Most High, and praised and honoured the one who lives for ever' (and Daniel refers to God as 'the one who lives for ever' in 12:7).

Daniel speaks

Although Daniel is a key character in this story, he has so far not spoken at all. Indeed, in the whole of chapter 6 the words in verses 21 and 22 are the only ones he speaks. His opening words are notable, especially in light of Darius's reference to 'the living God': 'O king, live for ever!' (v. 21). Elsewhere in Daniel, the Aramaic word for 'living/to live' is used a number of times with reference to the king. In 2:4 and 3:9 the Chaldeans say to Nebuchadnezzar, 'O king, live for ever!' Then, in 5:10 the queen says the same thing to

Belshazzar, and in 6:6 the presidents and satraps say, 'O King Darius, live for ever!' On each occasion, with the probable exception of the queen's speech, the sincerity of the words is rather dubious. In Daniel's speech, however, they certainly appear genuine and provide evidence of his appropriate reverence (within the boundaries allowed by his 'faithful service' of God) for the king. Moreover, Daniel emphasizes that he has 'done no wrong' to the king—unlike the other rulers who earlier in the chapter said, 'O King Darius, live for ever' but then went on to trick him. Daniel immediately affirms that his salvation is God's doing (v. 22). Notably, he also affirms that he has been found blameless before God. Daniel is clearly a 'faithful servant' of some calibre!

The accusers are punished

The punishment of all 122 accusers plus their families has caused difficulty for many readers (v. 24). It seems a very harsh and unjust punishment, if not for the accusers themselves, then at least for their families. Such 'corporate' punishment does occur elsewhere in the Old Testament (see Numbers 16; Joshua 7; Esther 9:13, 25), and may be part of the cultural expectations of the time (although other parts of the Old Testament present a different picture: see, for example, Deuteronomy 24:16). Nonetheless, in general terms the punishment fits the crime along the lines indicated in Proverbs 28:10: 'Those who mislead the upright into evil ways will fall into pits of their own making.' Also, in terms of good storytelling, the exaggerated numbers (surely there were too many people—around 500—to fit in a lions' den), and the exaggerated ferocity of the lions who overpowered them 'before they reached the bottom of the den', demonstrate both the miraculous nature of Daniel's deliverance and the overwhelming triumph of 'good' over 'evil'.

PRAYER

Sovereign God, may our faithful service of you and,
so far as is appropriate, of others in authority have an impact on
those around us. May it help others to seek salvation from you
so that they too may serve you.

DARIUS' NEW DECREE

At the end of chapters 2, 3 and 4, King Nebuchadnezzar made statements that captured the main thrust of each of those chapters, and showed that he had learned the appropriate lesson. The lack of spoken response by Belshazzar fits with his character as revealed in chapter 5, and the bald statement, 'That very night Belshazzar, the Chaldean king, was killed' (5:30) may be intended to show that he hadn't learnt his lesson. Chapter 2 is about God giving Daniel the ability to interpret Nebuchadnezzar's dream, and at the end of the chapter the king says, 'Truly, your God is God of gods and Lord of kings and a revealer of mysteries' (2:47). Chapter 3 is about God delivering Shadrach, Meshach and Abednego from the fiery furnace, and Nebuchadnezzar says at the end, 'Blessed be the God of Shadrach, Meshach, and Abednego, who has sent his angel and delivered his servants who trusted in him' (3:28). Chapter 4 is about the ultimate sovereignty of God as opposed to the human sovereignty of even the great King Nebuchadnezzar; the king acknowledges this with the words, 'I blessed the Most High, and praised and honoured the one who lives for ever. For his sovereignty is an everlasting sovereignty, and his kingdom endures from generation to generation' (4:34). Darius' words at the end of chapter 6 similarly pick up the main theme from the chapter and demonstrate that the king here, too, has learnt his lesson. The construction of verse 25 seems intentionally to pick up on the start of chapter 4, and to build on the words found there.

In this way, Darius' words serve well as the final statement at the end of chapter 6, after which point the book of Daniel changes rather dramatically. The stories of Daniel and his three friends in the court of foreign kings now come to an end, to be replaced by Daniel's accounts of the strange visions he saw.

We noted earlier that some read verse 28 as equating Darius and Cyrus. It is more likely, however, that it is picking up on 1:21 and indicating that Daniel prospered beyond the period of Babylonian exile.

Commanded to worship

Darius may have learnt that Daniel's God is the living God whose kingdom never ends, who delivers and rescues, who works signs and wonders, but he is still seeking to use his own power to coerce others into worshipping (v. 26). Actually, very often in Christian history, people have 'converted' because someone in authority (whether a Roman emperor, a tribal chief, or the 'head' of the household) became a Christian and expected those under him (usually!) to do likewise, so perhaps we shouldn't be too critical of Darius here. Moreover, many people initially 'come to faith' under pressure, conscious or otherwise, from someone in authority (a parent, vicar or youth leader), or because of the faith of someone close to them. The ideal must surely be that people come to a faith of their own without obvious or hidden coercion, although many people do 'grow' into their own personal faith over time.

Key themes

Darius' proclamation draws together a number of key themes from the first half of the book of Daniel.

- Daniel's God is the living God who endures for ever.
- God's kingdom and dominion endure for ever. This may be the key theme in the book of Daniel as a whole.
- God delivers and rescues his people: Daniel's God is a God of salvation, and all the nations need to know it, even if issuing a command for them to worship this God is not the way to go about it!
- God works signs and wonders, even though Daniel and his friends were faithful when there was no certainty of God's miraculous intervention.

PRAYER

Sovereign God, help us to think through these four themes
from the book of Daniel and discern which of them are
most relevant for us at this moment.

DANIEL HAD *a* DREAM

Chapter 7 is key in terms of the overall shape of the book of Daniel. The chiastic structure of chapters 2—7 indicates that chapter 7 corresponds to chapter 2. Moreover, these chapters are all in Aramaic, while chapter 1 and chapters 8—12 are in Hebrew. They are also punctuated by reference to 'all/any peoples, nations and languages' (3:29; 4:1; 6:25; 7:14). This all seems to indicate that chapter 7 belongs with these earlier chapters, but the chronological sequence that runs through chapters 1—6 is disrupted in chapter 7, where we jump back to the first year of Belshazzar. (The following chapters are then set in the reigns of Belshazzar, Darius and Cyrus.) Moreover, chapters 7—12 are markedly different from the earlier chapters, as we discussed in the introduction. It may be, then, that chapter 7 is intended to be the 'hinge' between the two halves of the book, both connecting back to the stories in chapters 1—6 and also introducing the apocalyptic material.

The structure of chapter 7

The structure of chapter 7 itself is significant. Unlike earlier chapters, here the description of the dream and its interpretation form the bulk of the chapter: the dream is not set within a story as in chapters 2 and 4. The chapter starts with a one-verse introduction and ends with a one-verse conclusion. In between, it falls into two halves, the first half describing the dream and the second half its interpretation:

Introduction (7:1)
The dream (7:2–14)
The interpretation (7:15–27)
Conclusion (7:28)

The two halves between the introduction and conclusion then fall into four sections each, alternating between an earthly focus and a heavenly focus:

The dream:
On earth (7:2–8)
In the heavenly court (7:9–10)

On earth (7:11–12)
In the heavenly court (7:13–14)

The interpretation:
Daniel's request for information (7:15–16)
Heavenly attendant's response (7:17–18)
Daniel's request for information (7:19–22)
Heavenly attendant's response (7:23–27)

The alternation in the dream is demonstrated by an alternation between prose (for the sections set 'on earth') and poetry (for the sections set 'in the heavenly realm').

There is also a chiastic structure to the dream, which establishes the central focus of the dream as the throne scene in verses 9 and 10, and the conclusion as the appearance of 'one like a human being' (or, in other translations, 'like a son of man').

A Four creatures appear (7:2b–3)
  B The first three creatures (7:4–6)
    C The fourth creature (7:7)
      D The small horn (7:8)
        E The throne scene (7:9–10)
      D The small horn (7:11a)
    C The fourth creature (7:11b)
  B The first three creatures (7:12)
A 'One like a human being' appears (7:13–14)

He wrote down the dream

It is significant that Daniel writes down his dream. Elsewhere we read of prophecy being written down (Isaiah 8:1, 16; 30:8; Jeremiah 30:2; 36:2; 51:60; Ezekiel 43:11; Habakkuk 2:2). This emphasizes the importance of the dream and also indicates that it is recorded for future generations, which is significant because of the focus on future events in the second half of Daniel.

REFLECTION

How do you respond to the claim of Daniel that events on earth are closely linked with what happens in heaven? Does it make a difference to your belief and practice to know that God is sovereign in heaven and will eventually establish that sovereignty on earth also?

The FOUR GREAT BEASTS

These verses describe the first part of Daniel's dream, in which he sees four very strange beasts. Much scholarly energy has been invested in trying to work out what these beasts might represent, and what the background might be to the strange imagery. Some possible parallels have been found in Babylonian and Canaanite mythology, and it seems likely that the imagery in this chapter does pick up on the myths of other ancient Near Eastern civilizations. The imagery is put to very different use in Daniel, however, in the service of proclaiming the absolute sovereignty of the God of the Jews. Moreover, much of the imagery may well have its roots in Hebrew tradition (although, elsewhere in the Old Testament, use is made of images taken from Babylonian and Canaanite and other mythology, so Daniel may at times be drawing on something in the Jewish scriptures which has in turn drawn on other ancient myths). In particular, the mention of a lion, a leopard, a bear and a wild animal in Hosea 13:7–8 probably lies behind the imagery of the four beasts in Daniel, although in Hosea the animals are not deformed, and the images are applied to God.

Four winds of heaven and the great sea

'The four winds of heaven' (v. 2) appear again in 8:8 and 11:4. The number 'four' probably indicates completeness, and 'the four winds of heaven' may represent 'the power of God effecting his will' (Goldingay, p. 160). God is described earlier in Daniel as 'the God of heaven' (notably in 2:18, 19, 37, 44), 'God in heaven' (2:28), 'the King of heaven' (4:37), 'the Lord of heaven' (5:23), or just 'Heaven' (4:26). Also, Nebuchadnezzar heard a voice speaking to him from heaven (4:31) and later in chapter 7 we read of 'one like a human being coming with the clouds of heaven' (7:13).

By contrast, 'the great sea' or just 'the sea' may represent the antithesis of God, in this case 'primeval chaos'. It is true that elsewhere in the Old Testament the 'great sea' refers to the Mediterranean Sea, but even if that is the case here, it seems nonetheless to symbolize chaos or evil. Elsewhere in the Old Testament, the sea is the home of the monsters of chaos, Rahab and Leviathan (see Isaiah

27:1; 51:9; Psalm 74:13–14; 89:9–10). In the Old Testament, God is the creator who ordered all things and made them 'good'. The beasts represented here, which God caused to rise up out of the waters of chaos, are perversions of that good order and are therefore opposed to God and to God's intentions in creation.

The four beasts

There has been much dispute about what the beasts represent. Most scholars regard them as the four consecutive kingdoms of Babylon, Media, Persia and Greece; more conservative scholars argue that they are Babylon, Medo-Persia, Greece and Rome. The former seems more likely, partly because of the probable date when this material was written (during the Greek period), but more because the 'little horn' that springs up from the fourth beast is probably the Syrian ruler Antiochus IV Epiphanes, who ruled within the Greek empire (175–164BC). In fact, though, it doesn't matter too much in terms of the overall meaning of the passage, and what the beasts represent is probably not meant to be too precisely pinned down. The beasts are all deformed and grotesque. They are symbols of forces that arise against God—whatever those forces might be. Therefore, it is more significant that there are four of them (corresponding to the other 'fours' in the chapter) than that they be precisely identified with particular kings or kingdoms.

Whether the 'little horn' (v. 8) represents Antiochus IV Epiphanes or someone else, it symbolizes that which arrogates power to him/her/itself, arrogantly stands up to God and causes his people to suffer. It is the epitome of opposition to God, often summed up in the concept of an 'antichrist'.

REFLECTION

There are many things which might equate to these beasts in our society, such as the horrendously unfair distribution of resources that causes much of the world's population to face starvation while others live in wasteful luxury; oppressive regimes where Christians and others are appallingly treated because of their religious beliefs or ethnic background; the damage we are doing to God's creation through pollution, deforestation, killing off certain species of animals, and so on.

43

DANIEL 7:9–10

The ANCIENT ONE

As we move from the prose description of the four great beasts to the poetic portrayal of the divine court, there is a very stark change of tone. The horrifying picture of the grotesque beasts changes to a heavenly scene filled with light, peace and order.

This scene is one of a number of divine throne scenes in the Old Testament. Perhaps the most well-known is Isaiah 6, which starts, 'In the year that King Uzziah died, I saw the Lord sitting on a throne, high and lofty; and the hem of his robe filled the temple.' Ezekiel 1 is another example, filled with fantastic imagery which is similar in many respects to the imagery in Daniel. However, the plural 'thrones' in verse 9 may indicate that the divine council is in view here, whereby, drawing on ancient mythology, God is pictured as holding council with the heavenly beings in order to render judgment, as also found in Psalm 82 and Job. This would account for the 'thousand thousand' (v. 10) who serve him and the 'ten thousand times ten thousand' (in other words, a very large number) who attend him. Moreover, the end of verse 10 specifically states that 'the court sat in judgment' and, as we will see below, 'the books' that are opened are probably books of judgment. Pictured here is a judging God.

The ultimate judge

The 'Ancient One' is God, portrayed using imagery that probably has its background in Canaanite mythology. This mythology, it seems, provides appropriate images upon which Daniel's dream draws in order to capture the sense of the power and authority of God. Thus, in Canaanite mythology the divine assembly was headed by the high god, El, who is described as 'father of years' and has grey hair. El, too, faced the threat of chaotic forces associated with the sea (in the form of the sea-god Yamm), which he defeated. There are significant differences between the account in Daniel and the Canaanite myth, however: El's opponents were other gods, while God judges human kingdoms in Daniel; and while El's son, Baal (who, notably, is described as 'rider of the cloud': see Daniel 7:13), defeats his opponents in battle, in Daniel God seems simply to issue a word of judgment. It looks as though Daniel is 'demythologizing' popular myths in order to portray the Jewish God as the ultimate judge.

The clothing that 'was white as snow' (v. 9) may indicate either the splendour of God or the purity of God. Both would be relevant here. Fire, similarly, can mean different things: again it may represent God's majesty or it may be associated with judgment. Fire often accompanies the presence of God in the Old Testament, for example at the burning bush, as the Israelites wandered in the wilderness, or on Mount Sinai. The fiery throne with wheels which were 'burning fire' may be a picture of God riding in a flaming chariot. Its significance is that God is not static, but can move to where the people of God are, whether that be in Jerusalem or in exile in Babylon. This is similar to the vision in Ezekiel 1—3.

The books were opened

In addition to the books mentioned here (v. 10), we find also 'the book of truth' in 10:21 and another book, in which people's names are written, in 12:1. These books appear to be different from the others: here they appear to be records of people's (or nations') deeds for the purpose of judgment. There are hints of such records elsewhere in the Old Testament (Nehemiah 5:19; 13:14; Isaiah 65:6; Psalm 51:1; 109:14). This passage in Daniel emphasizes that God judges people and nations for their deeds. The beasts are held accountable, and there will also be a reckoning for the 'beastly' things in people and nations today. This doesn't correlate well with the picture held by some people of a God who will accept people just as they are and whatever they do, regardless of whether or not they show any sign of repentance. This passage portrays a God who takes evil deeds very seriously indeed, but does accept people just as they are and whatever they've done—providing they turn to God in repentance.

REFLECTION

Daniel's dream draws on symbolism that his first readers would have understood and uses it to convey important things about God, even though the source of the symbolism isn't in line with Jewish beliefs. What implications might there be for the language and images we use today, in order to convey to people who God is?

DOMINION REMOVED

We return now to the scene on earth. Indeed, verse 11 picks up exactly where verse 8 left off. It's as though we're flitting back and forth between two scenes, one on earth and one in heaven, which are both happening at the same time—and this is precisely the point: just as these monstrous things are taking place on earth, so God is responding in heaven. What occurs in this passage is the outworking of the implicit judgment of God (though not explicitly stated) in the preceding verses.

Arrogant words

The 'noise of the arrogant words' (v. 11) here picks up on the 'mouth speaking arrogantly' in 7:8, and we meet the expression 'a mouth that spoke arrogantly' again in 7:20. Although the Aramaic is literally 'much' (or 'many words') rather than 'arrogant' (NRSV) or 'boastful' (NIV), it is picked up again in 7:25, where we read of one who 'shall speak words against the Most High', which does seem to indicate arrogance or defiance of God. It appears that the worst crime committed by this individual (symbolized by the little horn) is that he defies God. As noted earlier, this horn probably represents the Syrian ruler Antiochus IV Epiphanes, who in 167BC stormed the temple in Jerusalem, defiled it and tried to stamp out Jewish religious practice. With Antiochus we meet the first record in history of specifically religious persecution (but see Esther 3); moreover, Antiochus, who called himself 'Epiphanes' meaning 'God manifest', is also the first Greek ruler to have taken a divine title for himself.

The beast was put to death

The worst of the beasts, the fourth, is put to death, 'its body destroyed and given over to be burned with fire' (v. 11b). Burning by fire was a punishment in the Old Testament for offences perceived as particularly heinous (see, for example, Genesis 38:24; Leviticus 20:14; 21:9; Joshua 7:15, 25). It is also a common way of describing divine punishment (see, for example, Isaiah 30:27–33; Ezekiel 28:18; Psalm 11:6).

However, it is not 'hell' as such that is pictured here, but rather the complete destruction of a particularly evil kingdom. This beast, which is so deformed that it cannot even be compared to a known animal, represents a kingdom that is no longer recognizable as an authority established by God. It must, therefore, be destroyed.

'For a season and a time'

Scholars have been puzzled by the fact that the lives of the first three beasts were prolonged, even after their dominion was taken away from them (v. 12). It is difficult to account for this historically (although Media and Persia did continue as two fairly independent principalities called Atropatian Media and Persis), but perhaps there are two key theological points being made, regardless of any possible historical background. First, the fourth beast is clearly portrayed as the worst, and it may be that the previous three, which still appear as recognizable animals, are not considered to have distorted their God-given role enough to be destroyed. Second, at times the prophets refer to an era in the future when Israel will rule over its former oppressors, which would suggest that these oppressive nations are not to be completely destroyed.

God's judgment is severe, but just. The differing treatment of the beasts indicates that there is a point at which God will intervene and destroy a kingdom which has so overreached its authority that it can no longer be regarded as 'instituted by God' (see Romans 13:1). But even kingdoms that clearly do not exercise their authority in line with God's will may be permitted to continue, so long as they have not completely distorted their God-given roles. The greatest crime against God seems to be an active defiance of God, so perhaps we should expect those nations whose leaders actively defy God to be overthrown.

REFLECTION

Perhaps we should be praying for the overthrow of governments where this takes place, confident that God will destroy those who defy him and persecute God's people. We should also search ourselves to see if there are ways in which we defy God.

One Like *a* Human Being

The main focus of these two verses, and the climax of the whole vision, is the 'one like a human being' (NRSV; or 'one like a son of man' in NIV). These verses have been the focus of more scholarly and other attention than any other part of the book of Daniel, so it is important, before we consider them in a little more detail, to give some attention to just who the 'one like a human being' (v. 13) is or represents.

Who is the 'one like a human being'?

Traditionally, both in Jewish and Christian history, this individual has been seen as a messianic figure. Christians often relate this figure to Jesus' use of the expression 'the Son of Man' and see it as a fore-shadowing, if not actually a foretelling, of Jesus himself. It should be made clear immediately, however, that while it seems likely that Jesus had the figure from Daniel in mind when he chose this title for himself, the expression in Daniel does not obviously function as a messianic title. Firstly, it is indefinite—'a son of man', not the defi-nite '*the* son of man'—suggesting that it is not a title as such. Secondly, the expression is 'one *like* a son of man', which indicates that whoever it is, the individual is likened to a human being rather than actually being a human being. Thirdly, this is symbolic language within a vision that includes clearly symbolic and unrealistic animals. 'Son of man' in Hebrew and Aramaic emphasizes the humanness of the individual, so the expression in the NRSV, 'one like a human being', is probably a good 'politically correct' way of rendering it. This also demonstrates that the 'humanness' of this individual is the focus, presumably by contrast with the deformed beasts representing evil kingdoms. That is to say, this figure is as God intended. The expression may also pick up on the concept of people being created in God's image in Genesis 1: this is God's true representative, and perhaps 'image'.

Nonetheless, most scholars expend a great deal of energy in trying to work out who this 'one like a human being' represents. The list includes a Davidic king, the second-century Jewish hero Judas Maccabeus, a future (messianic) Davidic king, a priestly figure or the high priest, the faithful ones within Israel, Israel itself, Daniel himself, a divine being or manifestation of God, angels, or specifically the angel Gabriel (see 8:16; 9:21; Luke 1:19, 26) or the angel Michael (see 10:13, 21; 12:1; Jude 9; Revelation 12:7). Opinion is split over whether it is a human or divine figure (partly depending on how 'coming with the clouds of heaven' is understood), and whether it is truly individual or an individual figure representing a collective. In the end, I find the archangel Michael, as the heavenly representative of the faithful believers on earth, to be the most convincing option—but I think the point is that there is really no definitive answer.

An enigmatic figure

All the figures in this dream, in fact, are somewhat enigmatic, and neither the dream itself nor the 'interpretation' specifically explain what or whom they represent. The ambiguity of the text should, I believe, be allowed to stand. While we may form our own opinions as to what each figure represents, in the end they should not be tied down, as this would restrict their further application in different situations. Besides, as Goldingay argues, 'Chap. 7 invites us to focus on the humanlike figure's role rather than its identity' (p. 172).

How does this relate to Jesus?

I have argued that the 'one like a son of man' does not represent Jesus, and that it is not, strictly speaking, messianic. As we reflect back on Daniel from a post-New Testament perspective, however, we can see how such a figure does foreshadow the hopes that Christians have of Jesus' reign when he comes again at the end of the age. In this sense, for Christians, the 'one like a human being' does point forward to Jesus, and this may well be part of the reason why Jesus seems to have chosen the rather enigmatic title 'the Son of Man' as his preferred self-designation.

REFLECTION

Does this seem to you a helpful way of finding Jesus as the 'fulfilment' of an Old Testament text?

46

To HIM WAS GIVEN DOMINION

Daniel's vision opened in 7:2 with the words, 'I, Daniel, saw in my vision by night…' The dream is then peppered with references to Daniel 'watching' (the same verb as 'saw' in Aramaic; the word occurs ten times in the chapter; see also 2:31, 34; 4:10, 13). The significance of the fourth beast is indicated by a repetition in 7:7 of the opening of the dream account: 'After this I saw in the visions by night a fourth beast…' Now the conclusion and climax of the dream is indicated by the third occurrence of the opening phrase. In verse 13 we read, 'As I watched in the night visions…' (in Aramaic, the expression in verse 13 is identical to 'I saw in the visions by night' in 7:7; 'I… saw in my vision by night' in 7:2 is almost identical). At this point we return again to the divine realm.

Coming with the clouds of heaven

The observation that the 'one like a human being' comes 'with the clouds of heaven' (v. 13) suggests the association of this individual with the heavenly realm. This is in stark contrast to the four beasts who 'came up out of the sea' (7:3)—that is, from the place of chaos, the antithesis of the heavenly realm. On a number of occasions in the Old Testament, clouds are associated with an appearance of God, perhaps most notably when the Lord went in front of the Israelites in the wilderness 'in a pillar of cloud' by day… and in a pillar of fire by night' (Exodus 13:21; see also Exodus 19:16; Leviticus 16:2; Psalm 68:4; 104:3; Isaiah 19:1; Nahum 1:3). However, the 'one like a human being' is not equated with God because 'he came to the Ancient One [that is, God] and was presented before him'. Here, too, Daniel seems to be drawing on Canaanite mythology, as well as other biblical texts. Baal is a subordinate god to the Canaanite chief god, El, and is described as 'rider of the clouds'; he does battle with the sea god, Yamm, and when he is victorious he is told, 'Take your everlasting kingdom, your eternal dominion.' (Lucas discusses in some detail how this might relate to Daniel 7; see pp. 173–6.) This command to Baal correlates with the key theme of Daniel 7:13–14, as the 'one like a human being' is given 'everlasting dominion' and 'kingship… that shall never be destroyed'.

Universal dominion

Daniel 7 strongly emphasizes that it is precisely to the 'one like a human being' that 'dominion' (repeated three times) and 'kingship' (repeated twice) will be given. Moreover, this dominion will be universal (over 'all peoples, nations and languages', the last occurrence of this phrase: see 3:4, 7, 29; 4:1; 5:19; 6:25), eternal ('his dominion is an everlasting dominion that shall not pass away') and powerful ('his kingship is one that shall never be destroyed') (v. 14). This universal, eternal and powerful dominion is contrasted with that of the beasts, which presumably seemed very widespread, rather long-lasting and pretty potent to those who suffered under their rule.

All people, nations and languages

The expression 'all people, nations and languages' has occurred repeatedly throughout the Aramaic section of the book of Daniel and constitutes something of a thread to tie these chapters together. This has led Lederach to describe 2:4b—7:28 as 'A Tract to the Nations'. He argues that this part of the book is designed to have relevance beyond the Jewish community. Thus its themes are universal and it is written in 'the tongue of culture and commerce'. Chapters 8—12, on the other hand, are written in Hebrew, and are concerned with issues of particular relevance to the Jews.

The meaning of the dream

Even if we can't pin down precisely who or what the various figures in the dream represent—most particularly, in this section, the 'one like a human being'—the main point of the dream remains the same: God will remove the power of those who are depraved (presumably in the sense that they do not function as God intended) and give it to one who functions as God intended. That one will be given sovereignty and will exercise universal, eternal and powerful dominion on God's behalf.

PRAYER

Sovereign God, bring about your universal, eternal and powerful dominion on earth—especially within me!

THEY SHALL POSSESS *the* KINGDOM

The description of the dream seems to be over, but we are given a few additional details about it in later verses. This seems to imply that what we are given in 7:2–14 is an abbreviated version of the dream, which adds to the caution we should exercise in trying to pin it down too precisely. Moreover, although 'one of the attendants' provides some interpretation of the dream, it is by no means exhaustive: many details are left unexplained.

My spirit was troubled

Daniel's reaction to the dream (v. 15) is typical of what we find elsewhere in the book (see 2:1; 4:5; 5:6; 8:27). Why Daniel responded in this way is unclear. Perhaps it was because he didn't understand the dream, but that wouldn't explain why, in 7:28, after he has received the interpretation, he still says, 'My thoughts greatly terrified me, and my face turned pale.' We will consider this further when we get to 7:28; for now, we might consider two possible explanations for Daniel's response. First, he has experienced a terrifying dream which he doesn't understand, and second, he may perceive that he has had an insight into heavenly things.

The holy ones of the Most High

The identity of 'the holy ones' (v. 18) has generated almost as much debate among scholars as the phrase 'one like a human being'. As Collins notes, 'Traditionally, the holy ones have been identified as human beings—the "saints" by Christians and the Jewish people by Jews' (pp. 312–3). Indeed, the KJV (and the NKJV) and the RSV (but not the NRSV), as well as the Jewish Old Testament in English (JPS, but not the latest edition), use the word 'saints' here. The debate among recent scholars is over whether they represent human beings or angelic beings. The majority view is that 'the holy ones' represent angelic beings, but that 'the people of the holy ones of the Most High' in 7:27 are the Jews, or faithful Jews, like 'the holy people' in 12:7. This is based on the observation that the vast majority of references to 'holy ones' elsewhere in the Bible (for example, Job 5:1; 15:15; Psalm 89:5, 7) and beyond refer to angelic beings, and the other uses of the word in Daniel certainly do so (see 4:13, 17, 23; in 4:8, 9, 18 and 5:11 we meet the expression 'the holy God/gods', and these are the only other occurrences of the Aramaic word 'holy [one(s)]' in the book). Redditt points out that in 7:25 'the holy ones' are given over into the power of the little horn (Antiochus?) and argues that 'it seems implausible that Daniel 7 portrayed an attack on angels by Antiochus' (p. 128). It is likely, however, that Redditt, along with many other commentators, has fallen into the trap of trying to pin down the imagery too precisely—imagery designed to be allusive and to capture by means of pictorial language important theological truths that relate to events in the second century BC, but are not exhausted by such events. I agree with Goldingay that 'the trouble with Daniel 7 is that it does not say *anything* unequivocally about the identity of the holy ones', so that, just as with 'the one like a human being' it is inevitable that people will come to different conclusions.

The point of the symbolic imagery

So what is the point of all this? Firstly, Daniel emphasizes that the earthly and heavenly realms are intimately intertwined, such that it is impossible to separate what happens in one from what happens in the other. There are spiritual dimensions to the things that happen on earth. Secondly, God's eternal kingdom will be given to those considered holy by God—whether angelic or human, or (probably) both. Thirdly, many people have made a meal of Daniel (and similarly the book of Revelation) because they have tried too hard to pin down the symbolism. It is the nature of this type of literature that it refuses to yield to nice, neat interpretation. Rather, its enduring value derives from the fact that it resonates in many very different situations. It conveys theological truth through symbols that can be applied to many different people, nations and situations, whatever the author had specifically in mind when he wrote it (or, perhaps, whatever Daniel had in mind when he dreamed it, or God had in mind when God inspired it).

REFLECTION

How do you react to this kind of literature? Do you find it helpful, inspiring or infuriating?

The FOURTH BEAST & ITS HORNS

In this section and the next, the interpreting angel specifically answers
Daniel's request 'to know the truth concerning the fourth beast... and
concerning the ten horns... and concerning the other horn' (7:19–20).
The information given is sparse, however, and does little to provide a
definitive historical interpretation of these things.

The fourth beast

As we noted earlier, the majority of scholars maintain that the fourth
beast (v. 23) refers to the Greek empire. Many conservative scholars,
though, maintain that it is the Roman empire, some arguing that this
'Roman empire' extends to the present day and will continue until the
'end times'. This interpretation is partly because they see the dream as
'predicting' Jesus and the end times described in the New Testament.
Certainly it is pictured as an empire of a different order from those that
preceded it, and this would be equally true for Jews living in the Greek
period under, say, Antiochus IV, or Jews living in the Roman period, say
around the time of the destruction of the temple in AD70 (or followers
of Jesus around the time of his death). But it could be, and has been,
applied to later 'empires' as well.

The majority of scholars view the 'ten horns' (v. 24) as ten Syrian
(Seleucid) kings leading up to Antiochus IV, although they disagree
over precisely which ten kings they are! The three horns may then be
three people whom Antiochus had to overcome in order to obtain the
throne—perhaps Seleucus IV who preceded him, and the sons of
Antiochus III (who preceded Seleucus IV), Antiochus and Demetrius.
Many conservative scholars regard the ten and the three horns as
kings/kingdoms within the Roman empire, although the horns have
also been linked to all sorts of people or kingdoms or organizations in
more recent times (like, for example, the ten nations that once made
up the Common Market—now the European Union, with far more
than ten members).

The little horn

As we have noted, most scholars understand the 'little horn' to refer to
Antiochus IV, who is regarded as fulfilling very well what is said about it

in verse 25. In 167BC he sent an army to attack Jerusalem, deliberately entering the city on the sabbath, when faithful Jews would not fight. Many Jews were slaughtered, the temple was desecrated and a decree was issued that sought to end all Jewish practices. Many sacred books were burned and the Jews were even prevented from reading the law. Circumcision was banned, sabbath observance prohibited and all Jewish worship curtailed. Indeed, Jews were commanded to sacrifice pigs, a taboo animal, and they were forced to eat ritually unclean food.

More conservative scholars regard the little horn as some kind of anti-christ figure, along the lines of what we find in the book of Revelation.

For a time, two times and half a time

The expression 'for a time, two times and half a time' (v. 25) has usually been understood to mean three and a half years, and is calculated roughly as the period from when Antiochus desecrated the temple in 167BC to his death in 164 or to the rededication of the temple in the same year (see also 8:14; 12:11–12; 1 Maccabees 4:54). The apparent exactness doesn't fit well in the context, however, and it is not exact anyway because this actual time period was just over three years. Moreover, the phrase literally means 'for a time, *times* and half a time', which doesn't necessarily suggest three and a half years. Probably, it indicates that the reign of the one represented by the little horn will be for a restricted period only, and not for ever as is the case with the kingdom given to the holy ones in 7:18 and 22.

People have a great hunger to know about the future. Throughout Jewish and Christian history, people have tried to relate the imagery and the numbers in Daniel to events in history or within their own lifetimes. Predictions have also been made about events in the future, sometimes giving very precise dates for when, for example, Christ will return, based on calculations using the numbers in Daniel. While Daniel does give strong assurances that wicked dominions will be destroyed and that God will give an eternal kingdom to 'the holy ones', the book does not reveal precise details about the future. This, it seems, is not for people to know.

REFLECTION

How do you respond to the combination in Daniel of firm assurances that the future is in God's control and allusive imagery portraying just what will happen in the future?

An EVERLASTING KINGDOM

We noted earlier that the dream reached a climax with the appearance of 'one like a human being', but a particular emphasis in chapter 7 as a whole is on the new kingship (or kingdom) which is given to the 'one like a human being' in verse 14, to 'the holy ones of the Most High' in verses 18 and 22, and to 'the people of the holy ones of the Most High' in verse 27. Thus, although the appearance of the 'one like a human being' is central, the chapter moves on from that centre to focus on the kingdom. It seems that this new kingdom is initiated with the arrival of the 'one like a human being'.

The court shall sit in judgment

We might also note that chapter 7 moves three times from description of the fourth beast, which is different from all the rest, to consideration of the ten horns, to a focus on the little horn that displaces three of those horns and speaks arrogantly, to divine judgment being given, and finally to the giving of a new kingdom. This might suggest that the fourth beast and particularly the little horn represent something that the original readers could be expected to relate to personally, especially if it represented an oppressive regime under which those readers were suffering. The promise for the readers is that judgment will be meted out, the kingdom will be removed from the oppressor (or from any such oppressor), and dominion will be established in the hands of those associated with God.

Kingship and dominion

It is clear from the repetition within this section that 'kingship' or 'kingdom' (the same word in Aramaic, occurring four times in these verses), and 'dominion' (occurring three times), are key themes. The words are not quite identical: 'kingship' means either 'realm' or 'rule', whereas 'dominion' relates to 'having mastery' or 'having sovereignty'. Both are key themes in Daniel, but 'kingship/kingdom' occurs throughout most of the book (though less in chs. 8—11 and not at all in ch. 12), while 'dominion' occurs only in chapters 2—7 (the Aramaic section of the book). The refrain in chapter 4, which is also picked up in chapter 5, uses both words and gives some sense of the difference between them: 'the Most High has sovereignty [dominion] over the kingdom of mortals and gives it to whom he will' (4:17, 25, 32; 5:21). 'Sovereignty' here is the same word as 'dominion' in 7:26–28. The point here, and in the rest of chapters 2—7, is that ultimately both 'kingship' and 'sovereignty' lie with God, and God has the power to determine who should exercise kingship and sovereignty.

The kingship/kingdom and sovereignty of God are two key themes (if not *the* two key themes) in the book of Daniel. The concept of 'kingdom' or 'kingship' occurs more in Daniel than anywhere else in the Old Testament, and Daniel was almost certainly a crucial book in Jesus' and the New Testament writers' formulation of the concept of 'the kingdom of God'. 'The kingdom of God' is perhaps the key element in Jesus' teaching, where, just as in Daniel, it has present ramifications as well as providing hope for the future when God's rule will be fully established on earth. We see the presence of God's 'kingdom/kingship' in Daniel and his friends, but chapter 7 also makes clear that at some point in the future all other sovereignty will give way to God's sovereignty and his kingdom will 'come' in all its fullness. Moreover, whatever the original meaning of the 'one like a human being', the picture in chapter 7 of a new kingdom being initiated with this individual does seem to foreshadow the coming of the kingdom with Jesus in the New Testament.

PRAYER

Sovereign God, help us to see the present signs of your rule on earth and to work towards your kingdom being fully established in the future.

50

HERE *the* ACCOUNT ENDS

The chapter comes to a very abrupt ending, especially when compared to the previous chapters, most of which finish with a summarizing conclusion, often from the mouth of the foreign king. Chapter 7, by contrast, starts with a one-verse introduction, devotes almost all of the rest of the chapter to a description of Daniel's vision, then closes with one verse which begins, 'Here the account ends' (v. 28). There is no explanation, but just a note to tell us that once again Daniel is left terrified. Before we get to that abrupt ending, however, we encounter 'the people of the holy ones of the Most High' (v. 27).

The people of the holy ones

We noted earlier that the majority scholarly opinion is that 'the holy ones of the Most High' (7:18, 21–22, 25) refers to heavenly beings, and that 'the people of the holy ones of the Most High' here refers to Jews. This may be correct. On the other hand, Goldingay argues that 'the holy ones', 'the holy ones of the Most High', and 'the people of the holy ones of the Most High' all refer to the same group, and that 'Dan 7 is too allusive to enable us to decide with certainty whether the holy ones are celestial beings, earthly beings, or both' (p. 178). Seow goes further and argues that the 'one like a human being' also represents the same group: 'God's angelic hosts' and 'God's terrestrial host' (p. 110). I suspect that the 'one like a human being' does represent an individual, that the 'holy ones' are angels and that 'the people of the holy ones' are just that: people. But it is allusive, and the reader is probably supposed to see very close links between all three. They are all on the same side, fighting the same battle, whether that be at God's side, in the heavenly places or on earth. Nonetheless, it is very significant that the 'dominion' and the 'kingship', which were given to 'one like a human being' (7:13–14), will eventually pass on to 'the people of the holy ones of the Most High'. This suggests that, in due time, God's people will inherit his kingdom. Moreover, this kingdom was earlier portrayed as universal, eternal and powerful. The universal aspect is picked up here by the phrase 'all dominions shall serve and obey them' (v. 27). The eternal aspect is reiterated here too—'their kingdom shall be an everlasting kingdom'

—and the 'greatness of the kingdoms under the whole heaven' conveys its power.

'My thoughts greatly terrified me'

At the end of his dream, with its insights into the heavenly realm, Daniel, like Belshazzar in chapter 5, is 'greatly terrified' and his 'face turned pale'. His terror may be because of the dreadful things he has seen; it may be because he has had an encounter with heavenly beings; it may be because of the oppression that still lies in the future, before God intervenes; or it may be because he doesn't understand all that he has seen. The text doesn't make it clear. Nonetheless, Daniel's terror is clearly different from that of Belshazzar. Daniel is not the object of the vision he has seen, and is not due to be dealt with as Belshazzar was. Indeed, the observation that Daniel 'kept the matter in mind' indicates that he continued to reflect on it and probably continued to work out the implications for himself and his people. It is significant that the chapter ends with these words because it shows that Daniel's terror is not the end of the story— much as Mary's pondering in her heart what the shepherds told her about the angels' appearance was clearly not the end of her story (Luke 2:19). In both cases the individual didn't understand what was going on, but kept the matter in mind for a future time.

There are many aspects of Christian life and faith that we may not understand. There may even be aspects of life and faith that scare us. Nevertheless, we should remember that we are part of the people of God, and we should pray that we are able to keep in mind those matters that we don't understand and those things that scare us, until such time as we are able to deal with them properly. Perhaps, in some cases, that time won't be in this life!

PRAYER

Sovereign God, give us the strength to cope with those things we don't yet understand, the patience to ponder them in our hearts until such time as we do, and the grace to accept that there are things we will never understand in this life.

A Vision Like Ezekiel's

Daniel 8 is clearly intended as 'a companion piece' (Collins, p. 342) to chapter 7. The first verse of chapter 8 sets it around two years after the previous chapter, and the words 'a vision appeared to me, Daniel, after the one that had appeared to me at first' clearly link back to chapter 7. The overall structure of the two chapters is remarkably similar:

Introduction (7:1)	Introduction (8:1–2)
The dream (7:2–14)	The vision (8:3–14)
The interpretation (7:15–27)	The interpretation (8:15–26)
Conclusion (7:28)	Conclusion (8:27)

Moreover, both develop in roughly the same way. Starting with animals representing different kingdoms, they then home in on a number of horns on the last or latter of the animals, before narrowing the focus to one 'little horn' which constitutes the climax of the animal dream/vision. Both involve heavenly attendants who provide interpretations of the dream/vision. At the end of both, Daniel is left greatly shaken by the experience. (Goldingay, p. 207, provides a more detailed diagram showing some of these links.)

Differences between chapters 7 and 8

There are also some notable differences between the two. Firstly, chapter 8 is in Hebrew, while chapter 7 is the final chapter in Aramaic. There is no obvious reason for this change, but a number of commentators suggest that it may go along with the narrower focus on Jewish concerns which we find in chapters 8—12. There is a much greater and more explicit emphasis in this chapter on events that took place in Jerusalem in the 160s BC (under Antiochus IV Epiphanes), while earlier chapters were more concerned with life in exile, and, as we have seen, referred regularly to 'all peoples, nations, and languages'. Secondly, the interpretation of the vision is much more specific than in chapter 7. In the previous chapter, everything was decidedly allusive; here the two animals are specifically identified with Medo-Persia and Greece, and although the 'little horn' is not named, it is quite clearly (and almost all commentators agree that it is) Antiochus IV Epiphanes. In addition, the description of this 'little horn' fits very well with information we have from elsewhere (mostly 1 and 2 Maccabees) about Antiochus. Thirdly, although we encounter heavenly beings in chapter 8, we don't have the same alternation between the earthly and heavenly realms that characterized chapter 7. That alternation seems to have been one of the main points about chapter 7: the point is made and doesn't need to be reiterated here. There are other significant differences of detail, some of which we will note in later sections.

Goldingay describes chapter 7 as an 'impressionistic painting open to several interpretations' and chapter 8 as a 'political cartoon' (p. 201). This is helpful. As we have already seen, Daniel consists of very different types of literature. The stories in chapters 1—6 are obviously different from the visions in chapters 7—12, yet even two superficially similar chapters like 7 and 8 turn out to function in quite different ways.

I saw myself in Susa

Daniel is in Babylon during the reign of Belshazzar, some time around 550BC. In his vision he sees himself in Susa, one of the capitals of the Persian empire at a later stage: indeed, Goldingay states that 'Susa was in Jewish thinking *the* seat of the Persian empire (Nehemiah 1:1; Esther 1:2)' (p. 208). It seems that it was only in his vision that Daniel was located in Susa, and in this respect his vision is much like Ezekiel's, where Ezekiel is 'transported' from Babylon to Jerusalem (Ezekiel 8:3). Many commentators remark that Daniel 8 draws on the visions of Ezekiel (and we will see later that chapter 9 draws on Jeremiah).

PRAYER

Sovereign God, the capital cities of modern-day empires
are also very important places. We pray that people in these cities
may hear you speaking to them and that they may display more of
your sovereignty.

The RAM & the GOAT

This vision starts by describing two animals (vv. 3, 5). If the majority of scholars are right, the two animals here are represented by three animals in chapter 7, although none of the animals correlate. In addition, these animals are domestic, clean animals, while those in chapter 7 are deformed, monstrous animals. These may be arguments against the scholarly consensus, or they may simply indicate that chapter 7 is deliberately allusive, while chapter 8 is more concrete.

The ram with two horns

Chapter 8:20 will make it clear that the ram represents the Medo-Persian empire which took control of Palestine in about 539BC, seizing it from the Babylonians, who had attacked Jerusalem in 587, destroyed the city and the temple and exiled many Israelites. The ram was the Babylonian sign of the zodiac used to represent Persia, so it is an appropriate symbol here. Furthermore, the Persians often used the ram motif in their architecture. The two horns (v. 3) represent the kings of Media (perhaps Darius the Mede) and Persia (perhaps Cyrus). The horn is used elsewhere in the Old Testament as a sign of strength (see 2 Samuel 22:3; Psalm 18:2), and the length of these horns probably indicates military prowess. Hence, the longer horn, representing Persia, eventually overcomes the shorter horn, representing Media. The charging ram (v. 4) represents the spread of the Persian empire: 'westwards and northwards and southwards' indicates the extent of this spread, 'eastwards' being omitted probably because, from a Jewish perspective, Persia itself was the east.

The goat with one horn

Chapter 8:21 specifies that the goat represents the Greek empire, with Alexander the Great as the single horn. The Seleucids, the Greek rulers of Syria after the death of Alexander, were represented by the zodiac sign of Capricorn, the horned goat. The Greek empire originated in the west, relative to Palestine, and must have seemed to take over the whole world. The phrase 'coming across the face of the whole earth without touching the ground' (v. 5) indicates its extensiveness and also the speed with which the empire was established.

Between 334 and 331BC, Alexander won a series of decisive battles against the Persians (hence 'the ram did not have power to withstand it', v. 7) and established an empire that extended from Greece to India. The words in verse 8, 'but at the height of its power, the great horn was broken', correlate with Alexander's sudden death from a fever in 323BC, when he was only 33 years old. Following Alexander's death, his empire was divided among four of his generals, along geographical lines: hence, 'in its place there came up four prominent horns towards the four winds of heaven' (v. 8).

'Greatness' and the 'power'

'Greatness' and 'power' are important words in this section (and later in the chapter), emphasized by repetition. Thus the ram 'became *strong*' in verse 4; the goat 'grew exceedingly *great*' in verse 8; and also in verse 8 we read of 'the *great* horn' (all the same Hebrew word). In the next section we will read that the little horn became 'exceedingly great', that 'it grew' and then that it 'acted arrogantly', and each of these phrases uses the same Hebrew word. The passage thus describes increasing greatness and, by implication, the increasing arrogance that goes along with it.

The word 'power' occurs four times in this section in the NRSV, but only three times in Hebrew (one of which is rendered by 'force' in the NRSV). The three occurrences in Hebrew are '[the goat] ran at [the ram] with savage *force*' in verse 6; and 'the ram did not have *power* to withstand' and 'there was no one who could rescue the ram from its *power*' in verse 7. Here the power of Alexander the Great is repeatedly emphasized, as it is again in 8:22. The expression 'power to withstand' should be noted: the same expression occurs in 1:4 where Daniel and his friends are described as 'competent to serve' (the same words in Hebrew) in the king's palace. The fact that these same words are used of Daniel and his three friends as early as 1:4 already indicates that there are ways for faithful people to withstand the power of oppressive regimes.

REFLECTION

Can you think of ways in which God may give Christians today the power to withstand oppressive regimes, or to withstand the more subtle and perhaps insidious powers exerted by materialistic Western democracies?

The LITTLE HORN

The vision in chapter 8 comes to a climax with the 'little horn'. There is general agreement that the little horn represents Antiochus IV Epiphanes, who ruled Syria and Palestine (as part of the Greek empire) from 175 to 164BC. This means that there is quite a time gap between the 'four horns' in 8:8 (about 323BC) and the 'little horn' in verse 9. This gap will be filled in chapter 11.

Grew exceedingly great

Verse 9 informs us that the little horn 'grew exceedingly great'. Verse 10 then states that it 'grew as high as the host of heaven' and verse 11 that it 'acted arrogantly'. All three of these phrases, in Hebrew, use the verb 'to be great', bringing to a climax the use of the same verb earlier in the chapter. This also picks up on the references to the arrogance of the little horn in 7:8, 11 and 20. We noted earlier that Antiochus desecrated the temple in Jerusalem (alluded to in v. 13: 'the transgression that makes desolate, and the giving over of the sanctuary and host to be trampled'), that he tried to stamp out Jewish religious practice, including 'the regular burnt offering' mentioned here, and that he prohibited reading of the Torah—which is probably what lies behind 'cast truth to the ground' in verse 12.

The 'greatness' of Antiochus didn't just extend horizontally, 'towards the south, towards the east, and towards the beautiful land' (a reference to Israel; see also 11:16, 41). It also extended vertically as he, whether knowingly or not, challenged the 'host of heaven', the celestial army of God, and even 'the prince of the host', God. This shows that Antiochus' greatness had implications not just on earth but also in heaven. As he used his power not just to conquer other nations but also to subdue the religious practice of the Jews and to oppress the Jewish people, so his 'greatness' became a direct challenge to the God of the Jews.

How long?

The 'holy ones' who converse in verse 13 must be angels. They ask a question which is probably the key question in the whole chapter: 'How long?' They are asking, in effect, 'How long will this dreadful situation continue?' This is a question that occurs a number of times in the Old Testament when people are experiencing suffering or persecution (see, for example, Psalm 13; Isaiah 6:11).

'The transgression that makes desolate'

'The transgression that makes desolate' (v. 13) seems to be a play on the title *Ba'al Samen* ('desolate' is from the same root as 'Samen'), which was an Aramaic form of Zeus Olympius, the god for whom Antiochus set up an altar in the Jerusalem temple. This is seen as the ultimate challenge to the God of the Jews, and is picked up by the phrase 'an abomination that desolates' in 9:27; 11:31 and 12:11. It is also picked up in Jesus' words, 'So when you see the desolating sacrilege standing in the holy place, as was spoken of by the prophet Daniel...' (Matthew 24:15; Mark 13:14). 'Transgression' in verse 13 is the same word as 'wickedness' in verse 12, and it is picked up again in 8:23: 'when the transgressions have reached their full measure'.

1150 days?

The same kinds of issues arise in relation to the 'two thousand three hundred evenings and mornings' (v. 14) as for the 'time, two times and half a time' in 7:25. This time period is usually understood to be 1150 days, with '2300' referring to the total number of evening and morning sacrifices. This gives a figure of just under the three and a half years that 'a time, two times and half a time' is taken to indicate, so if chapter 8 was written a little later than chapter 7, they might be indicating the same period of time. However, the phrase 'evening and morning' usually refers to a single day, so the figure may mean 2300 days. This is somewhere under seven years and might be roughly equivalent to the 'week' (usually taken as seven years) in 9:27. Alternatively, it may be intended as a symbolic number indicating a restricted period of time rather than any precise period. This last approach seems to me to be the best one, given our inability to pin the time period down with any certainty.

PRAYER

Sovereign God, help us to avoid becoming arrogant or self-satisfied.
May we always remember our need for you.

54 DANIEL 8:15-17

GABRIEL APPEARS

Divine 'messengers' (the Hebrew word often translated as 'angel' simply means 'messenger') appear quite a number of times in the Old Testament, often specifically as 'the angel of the Lord'. The word is not used in the Hebrew parts of Daniel, although the Aramaic equivalent occurs twice. Once Nebuchadnezzar refers to the angel sent to Shadrach, Meshach and Abednego in the fiery furnace (3:28), and once Daniel relates that God sent an angel to shut the lions' mouths in the den (6:22). Angels are usually referred to as 'holy ones' in Daniel, but only in this book of the Old Testament are angels given names—Gabriel in 8:16 and 9:21, and Michael in 10:13, 21 and 12:1. Both these angels appear again in the New Testament, Gabriel in Luke 1:19, 26, and Michael in Jude 9 and Revelation 12:7.

'Having the appearance of a man'

Gabriel is described here as 'having the appearance of a man' (v. 15). His name means something like 'man of God' or perhaps 'warrior of God', and when he reappears in 9:21 he is described as 'the man Gabriel'. God's 'messengers' often appear in human form, so sometimes it is difficult, if not impossible, to tell whether they are meant to be seen as celestial beings or human. We might recall that 7:13 referred to 'one like a human being', who appears to be a heavenly being, and we should also note again the difficulty that commentators have in deciding if 'the holy ones of the Most High' in chapter 7 are angelic or human. Furthermore, when Nebuchadnezzar saw the 'angel' (his word, not the narrator's) in the fiery furnace with the three Jews, he initially said, 'I see four *men* unbound, walking in the middle of the fire', although he then added that 'the fourth has the appearance of a god' (3:25). Angels appear often in Zechariah 1—6; there they serve a similar function as in Daniel, in terms of helping the visionary to understand what he is seeing. Ezekiel, too, is assisted by celestial beings, although they are never described as 'angels'. Ezekiel himself is often referred to as 'son of man' ('mortal' in the NRSV) to emphasize his humanity, and the same happens here with Daniel in verse 17. Thus, while the celestial beings may have the appearance of human beings, it is emphasized that Daniel actually is a human being. Again, a close connection is established between the divine and human realms, although a clear distinction between them is also maintained.

Angels feature often in apocalyptic literature, much more so in later material than in Daniel. The references to divine messengers in Daniel, elsewhere in the Old Testament and also in the New Testament raise questions, however, about what angels are and whether we might expect to encounter them today. Throughout the Bible, it seems that God communicates with people through specially appointed messengers. Some of these are portrayed as celestial beings, some are clearly human, and sometimes it is not clear whether they are divine or human. It seems to me that we should expect the same today. There may be occasions when God's messengers are supernatural, although I suspect that this will be the exception rather than the rule.

'Help this man understand the vision'

Gabriel's task here (like that of the angels in Zechariah and Ezekiel) is to help Daniel understand his vision. 'Understanding' is the key theme of this short passage: Daniel's immediate response to the vision is 'When I, Daniel, had seen the vision, I tried to understand it' (v. 15). Gabriel is then instructed by 'a human voice' (presumably God's) to 'help this man understand the vision'. Gabriel says to Daniel, 'Understand, O mortal, that the vision is for the time of the end.' 'The time of the end' here seems, given its context, to refer specifically to the end of Antiochus' oppression of the Jews, rather than to some eschatological 'end'—although some scholars think that it refers to this also, and that the two are seen in Daniel as being synonymous. Next time we meet Gabriel (9:21–23), his task is somewhat similar: he says, 'Daniel, I have now come out to give you wisdom and understanding.' A feature of apocalyptic visions is precisely that they are beyond human understanding. Typically, interpreting angels are on hand to explain, but nonetheless there continue to be elements of the visions which are baffling and invite speculation about how they are to be understood or 'fulfilled'.

PRAYER

Sovereign God, help us to recognize your messengers (celestial or human) when we encounter them, and may we also be ready to be your messengers ourselves when you call us to that role.

55

The APPOINTED TIME of the END

These verses are the first part of Gabriel's explanation to Daniel of his animal vision. The interpretation of the vision falls into two parts. Verses 20–22 explain that the ram with the two horns represents the Medo-Persian empire, and that the goat with the great horn represents Greece under Alexander the Great, which was then divided among his four generals after his death. Verses 23–25 portray Antiochus IV Epiphanes, although he is neither named nor even explicitly referred to.

'I fell into a trance'

It seems rather surprising that the first thing Daniel does when Gabriel speaks to him is to fall asleep! The word translated 'trance' (v. 18) in the NRSV is literally 'deep sleep', but this is no ordinary sleep. The word is used of visionary experiences, as when Abram falls into 'a deep sleep' during a vision (Genesis 15:12), and the state is sometimes induced by God, as when God causes a 'deep sleep' to fall upon Adam before God makes the woman from his side (Genesis 2:21). The same thing happens to Daniel again in 10:9, where, again following a vision, he says, 'When I heard the sound of his words, I fell into a trance, face to the ground.'

'He touched me and set me on my feet'

The rousing or comforting touch of an angel is also a repeated part of Daniel's experience. Chapter 10:9, referred to above, is followed by the words, 'But then a hand touched me and roused me to my hands and knees.' We find something similar with Elijah in 1 Kings 19:5: 'Then he lay down under the broom tree and fell asleep. Suddenly an angel touched him and said to him, "Get up and eat."' Later in Daniel 10, an angel touches his mouth, which is like Isaiah's experience in Isaiah 6:7: 'The seraph touched my mouth with [the live coal]'. Something similar also happens in Jeremiah 1:9. In each case, the celestial being enables the prophet to speak.

Having touched Daniel, Gabriel then sets him on his feet (v. 18). 'Set me on my feet' is literally 'Stood me up on my standing place', and it picks up on the word 'stand, withstand, raise' that occurs twice in this chapter and often in chapter 11. The 'rising' of the kings in this section, and Antiochus' 'arising' in the next section, use the same word, and the same word was used earlier of 'withstanding' the rule of these kings. Gabriel, then, on God's behalf, gives Daniel the ability to 'stand', just as elsewhere God gives the ability to 'withstand'.

Part of the role of such angelic beings would appear to be to prepare people for what God has to say to them, or what he wants to do or say through them. This may involve cleansing, as in the case of Isaiah; or giving words to speak, as in the case of Jeremiah; or providing sustenance, as in the case of Elijah. In Daniel, it seems that comfort, strengthening and the gift of understanding are all aspects of the role of the angelic messenger. Of course, these may also be aspects of the role of God's human messengers.

The period of wrath

'Later in the period of wrath' (v. 19) should probably be rendered 'at the end of the period of wrath', because it uses the same word as 'at the end of their rule' in 8:23. Indeed, although elsewhere the word 'wrath' usually refers to the wrath of God, the 'period of wrath' probably indicates the same thing as 'their rule'—that is to say, the 'period of wrath' describes the rule of the kings portrayed in this vision. This means that 'the appointed time of the end', like 'the time of the end' in 8:17, indicates the end of the rule of the kings described here, particularly that of Antiochus IV Epiphanes, rather than the end of time as such. What is really significant, though, is that the time is 'appointed'. This means that God has set an end to Antiochus' reign, and this is probably the point also of the 'time, two times and half a time' in 7:25, and the 'two thousand three hundred evenings and mornings' in 8:14.

PRAYER

Sovereign God, thank you that you send your messengers, whether human or celestial or both, to comfort and strengthen us for the tasks you call us to undertake.

56 DANIEL 8:23–25

The LITTLE HORN BROKEN

Verses 23–25 constitute the climax of Daniel's vision. It is probably for this reason that the chapter changes at this point from prose to poetry: this is the only section of the chapter laid out in poetry, and the final two verses revert to prose. Antiochus is the one described as 'of bold countenance', which presumably picks up on the 'greatness' and 'arrogance' that we noted earlier. He is also described as 'skilled in intrigue' (v. 23, literally 'understanding riddles'), which shows that he was a very clever man. These two characteristics have been helpfully described as 'ruthless boldness' and 'artful cleverness' (Goldingay, p. 217), and these qualities form the focus of verses 24 and 25 respectively.

When transgressions reach full measure

The concept of the transgressions (of the Greek rulers and the empires they represent) 'reaching their full measure' (v. 23) seems a strange one, but it is not without biblical precedent. In Genesis 15:16 Abram is told that he cannot at that time possess the promised land because 'the iniquity of the Amorites is not yet complete'. Many people are disturbed by the fact that in the Old Testament the Israelites conquer a country that is already occupied, and are told by God to wipe out those who occupy the land (in Deuteronomy 7:1–6, for example). However, at least part of the explanation is that by Joshua's time the transgressions of those occupants, like those of the Greeks here, had 'reached their full measure'. The Israelite occupation of Palestine was partly judgment on the 'Amorites', just as the Assyrian occupation of the northern kingdom of Israel (in 722BC) was, at least in part, God's punishment of the Israelites, and the Babylonian occupation of Judah and Jerusalem (in 587BC) was the Judeans' punishment (see, for example, 2 Kings 17).

He shall grow strong in power

We noted earlier that the use and abuse of power is a key theme in chapter 8 and, indeed, in Daniel as a whole. Verse 24 describes Antiochus reaching the peak of his power and using it to wreak 'fearful destruction'. Where the NRSV says just, 'He shall grow strong in power', the Hebrew literally has, 'His power shall grow mighty, but not by his power'. NRSV omits 'but not by his power', taking it to be accidentally repeated from verse 22, but if it is original it indicates that the great power Antiochus had (and abused) ultimately came not from him but from God.

In his own mind he shall be great

The words 'in his own mind he shall be great' (v. 25) build on the references to 'greatness' earlier in the chapter (8:4, 8, 9, 10, 11 in Hebrew). They also represent the peak of Antiochus' arrogance: he was so sure of his own greatness that he even rose up against God (described as 'the Prince of princes'). 'Without warning he shall destroy many' is often taken as a reference to the surprise attack on Jerusalem described in 1 Maccabees 1:29–30, and this illustrates Antiochus's 'deceit'.

Not by human hands

It seems that Antiochus died in a military campaign in Persia late in 164BC, perhaps from some illness. The point being made by the last words of verse 25 is that Antiochus' reign came to an end because God ordained it so: the event was ultimately in God's control and not that of humans. It picks up on the stone made 'not by human hands' in Nebuchadnezzar's dream in chapter 2 (especially vv. 34, 45). There may also be an allusion to the violent resistance of the Maccabees. For Daniel, God is in control and his faithful people do not need to take matters into their own hands. The book, it seems, propounds a path of non-violent resistance.

The key message of Daniel is that however dreadful things may seem, however much oppressive rulers appear to be in control, ultimately God is in control and will fully establish his kingdom in due course. The book does portray faithful Jews resisting their oppressors, but it is always non-violent resistance, and it is always God who delivers them. By Antiochus' time, however, oppression had reached an unprecedented level. Specifically religious persecution was taking place, and many Jews were dying for their faith.

REFLECTION

Is there a time for violent resistance, or should we trust that when 'the transgressions have reached their full measure' God will intervene in some fashion?

SEAL UP *the* VISION

The vision and its interpretation are concluded. Gabriel now has a final few words to say to Daniel, and then we read of Daniel's response. Part of this response will, no doubt, come as no surprise by now: he says, 'I... was overcome and lay sick for some days' (v. 27).

It is true!

Gabriel affirms the truth of what Daniel has seen—specifically the 2300 evenings and mornings before 'the sanctuary shall be restored to its rightful state' (8:14). The restoration of the sanctuary was a key event: it symbolized that Jewish worship was again being properly conducted and indicated that God was again at the centre of Jewish life. It also symbolized the reversal of Antiochus' usurpation of power, and once the sanctuary was restored it gave the Jews confidence that the other things promised in Daniel's visions would be realized. The sanctuary was rededicated by Judas Maccabees in 164BC, the same year that Antiochus died. Similar affirmations of the truth of what is revealed to Daniel appear in 10:1 and 11:2 (see also Revelation 19:9; 21:5; 22:6).

For future generations

From the perspective of Daniel in the mid-sixth century BC, the events of Antiochus' reign in the first half of the second century were many, many years off. Hence, the written version of the vision is to be sealed up until such time as it makes sense to its readers—the oppressed Jews in the second century, suffering under Antiochus. Whenever Daniel 8 was actually written, the 'sealing up' of the vision indicates that it refers to things that are to happen in the future, and is to be preserved so that it might speak to future generations of the faithful, in the second century and beyond.

I lay sick for some days

Once again, Daniel's vision has quite an impact on him. This time, Daniel states, 'I was dismayed by the vision' (v. 27). The word 'dismayed' might be better translated 'appalled' or 'desolated': the word is from the same root as that used in 'the transgression that makes desolate' in 8:13, and the 'abomination that desolates' in 9:27 and 12:11. We should not minimize the suffering of the Jews under Antiochus. It was absolutely 'desolating', and it may be that Daniel's response to his visions is an indication of just how deeply shocking the situation was. Nor should we minimize the suffering that many believers have endured throughout history—including, of course, many in our own times.

I... did not understand it

'Understanding' was a key element in 8:15–17, and reappears here again at the end of the chapter. In chapter 1, Daniel was endowed with 'understanding' (1:4, 21), and it was stated that he had 'understanding' of all visions and dreams (1:17). Such understanding was demonstrated in chapters 2 and 4. In chapter 8, however, Daniel says that he is unable to understand the vision, so Gabriel comes specifically to help him understand (8:15–17), and a similar thing happens in 9:22–23 and 10:11–14. Even with Gabriel's help, though, Daniel still ends by saying, 'I... did not understand it.' Daniel, a man with a particular ability to understand dreams and visions and also helped to understand by a celestial messenger from God, does not understand the vision, so what chance is there of us being able to pin it down with any certainty? Some things, it seems, are beyond human understanding, even for those who have a particular gift of understanding and are assisted by God. So, for example, severe suffering experienced by innocent people may leave us feeling overcome and sick, and at a loss to understand. In the end, neither Daniel in particular nor the Bible in general enable us to grasp fully why God allows such suffering. Daniel does portray a God who ultimately is sovereign and will in the end act decisively to overthrow those who perpetrate such atrocities, but that may not necessarily make things any easier in the meantime.

PRAYER

Sovereign God, even when we see severe suffering that leaves us feeling sick and confused, help us to acknowledge your sovereignty and turn to you in faith.

JEREMIAH'S SEVENTY YEARS

Chapter 9 is quite different from the other chapters in Daniel for a number of reasons. Firstly, we don't find here the portrayal of faithful Jews responding to a threat from an oppressive king, as in chapters 1, 3 and 6. Nor do we find a dream or vision, as in the other chapters. Instead, the chapter reflects upon words in the book of Jeremiah, particularly his reference to 'seventy years' (v. 2). Secondly, most of the chapter consists of a long prayer by Daniel, the like of which we find elsewhere in the Old Testament (see 1 Kings 8:23–53; Ezra 9:6–15; Nehemiah 1:5–11; 9:6–37; Psalm 79 and also the apocryphal book of Baruch 1:15—3:8). Thirdly, chapter 9 uses very different language from the rest of Daniel, including the covenant name for God, Yahweh or the Lord (which isn't used at all elsewhere in the book), as well as terms characteristic of the book of Deuteronomy and literature particularly associated with it (which includes Solomon's prayer in 1 Kings 8 and also the book of Jeremiah).

The word of the Lord to Jeremiah

The central focus of this chapter is Daniel's efforts to understand Jeremiah's reference to the seventy years that 'must be fulfilled for the devastation of Jerusalem' (v. 2). Scholars are generally agreed that this refers to Jeremiah 25:11–12 and 29:10:

> *This whole land shall become a ruin and a waste, and these nations shall serve the king of Babylon seventy years. Then after seventy years are completed, I will punish the king of Babylon and that nation, the land of the Chaldeans, for their iniquity, says the Lord, making the land an everlasting waste... For thus says the Lord: Only when Babylon's seventy years are completed will I visit you, and I will fulfil to you my promise and bring you back to this place.*

The seventy years

Much time and effort has been invested in trying to pin down exactly what the seventy years refer to. In actual fact, Jerusalem fell to the Babylonians (under King Nebuchadnezzar) in 587BC; the Babylonian kingdom was then conquered by the Persians (under Cyrus) in 539BC, and the Persians allowed exiles to return to their home countries. This gives a period of some 48 years. However, Daniel 1:1 describes Jerusalem being besieged in 605, which would result in an 'exile' of around 66 years, close to the required seventy. Then again, the temple in Jerusalem, destroyed by the Babylonians in 587, was rebuilt from 520 to 515BC, so the period of the temple's destruction (587–515) gives 72 years, again close to seventy (and, indeed, some scholars date the destruction of the temple from 586 to 516). But does it really matter, and is this what Jeremiah meant anyway? I'm inclined to agree with those scholars who see 'seventy' as a round number indicating a normal human lifetime. In other words, Jeremiah was warning the Israelites that the generation going into exile in Babylon would not return from exile, arguing against the kind of optimism displayed by the prophet Hananiah (see Jeremiah 28), who stated that the exile would be over in two years. However it is understood, though, the final few verses of this chapter reinterpret the seventy years to give a much longer period of time, as we shall see later.

Beginning with scripture

We might note that where the NRSV has 'I, Daniel, perceived in the *books*', we could translate instead, 'I, Daniel understood from the *scriptures*'. (The word used might simply refer to documents, however, and could indicate letters from Jeremiah that had been preserved rather than meaning holy scripture as such. Indeed, in Jeremiah 29, his 'letter' is described using the same word found here.) In this chapter, Daniel is reflecting upon the significance of the prophet Jeremiah's words in relation to the events of his day. His reflection on this 'scripture' leads him into fervent prayer ('with fasting and sackcloth and ashes', v. 3), which eventually results in fresh understanding given by God. This is an excellent model for our use of the Bible, especially when we struggle to understand how it relates to our own circumstances.

REFLECTION

Is this a model for the use of scripture that you see reflected in your own experience, at least from time to time?

I Turned *to the* Lord

Having turned to 'scripture', Daniel then turns to the Lord in prayer. We need to consider precisely why he prayed (and I think the NRSV is a little misleading here), but first there is a historical detail to be dealt with.

In the first year of Darius

Like other chapters in Daniel, this one starts with an indication of when it is set, by giving the year of a particular king's reign. The king here is 'Darius son of Ahasuerus, by birth a Mede', who would appear to be the same Darius whom we meet in 5:31, chapter 6 and again in 11:1. We discussed the historical difficulties associated with this king earlier; here we note that he is described as 'son of Ahasuerus', another name for the Persian king Xerxes (the name used, for example, in the NIV). The name Ahasuerus is used only here in Daniel, once in Ezra (4:6) and throughout the book of Esther. If this is the same Darius and the same Ahasuerus that we know of from elsewhere, then there is a problem, because Ahasuerus was the son of Darius and not the other way around. Various solutions have been suggested (the most popular being that Ahasuerus was a throne name which might have been applied to any of the Medo-Persian kings), but in the end it remains a puzzle. Two important points should be noted here, though. Firstly, 'in the first year' (of Darius' reign) is repeated, thus adding emphasis. The significance is probably that this chapter is set at the time when the Babylonian empire (which had conquered Judah and Jerusalem and taken Israelites, including Daniel, into exile) was itself conquered, and 5:31 informs us that 'Darius the Mede' was the king to whom Babylon fell. Secondly, the verb that NRSV translates 'became king' is a passive form of the verb, which should be rendered 'was made king'. This seems a small point, but it is probably a hint that ultimately it is God who has set him up as king, in keeping with the words in 2:21 that it is God who 'deposes kings and sets up kings'.

Seeking God

The NRSV is unhelpful in verse 3. It renders the first part of the verse, 'Then I turned to the Lord God, *to seek an answer* by prayer and supplication.' The Hebrew text reads, 'I turned my face to the Lord God to seek (or plead) (with) prayer and petitions', which does not necessarily indicate that Daniel's reason for praying was 'to seek an answer'. Rather, Daniel, on behalf of the Israelites, seems to be doing exactly what is required by Solomon's prayer in 1 Kings 8:46–50:

> If they sin against you... so that they are carried away captive to the land of the enemy... and if they come to their senses... [and] repent with all their heart and soul... and pray to you... then hear in heaven your dwelling-place their prayer and their plea, maintain their cause and forgive your people who have sinned against you.

This also correlates with the words following the verse in Jeremiah 29 about 'Babylon's seventy years', to which we referred in the previous section.

> For thus says the Lord: Only when Babylon's seventy years are completed will I visit you, and I will fulfil to you my promise and bring you back to this place. For surely I know the plans I have for you, says the Lord, plans for your welfare and not for harm, to give you a future with hope. Then when you call upon me and come and pray to me, I will hear you. When you search for me, you will find me; if you seek me with all your heart.
> (Jeremiah 29:10–13)

Jeremiah 29:11 has been a significant verse for many people (including my wife and me), but often no account is taken of its context. The setting during the exilic period is very important, and Daniel picks up on this. But equally important is the exhortation to call upon the Lord and to seek the Lord with all your heart. Daniel does precisely this when he turns to the Lord, after reading, probably, this very section of Jeremiah. Thus the emphasis is not on seeking an answer, but on seeking God. Answers may come, but more important surely is finding God in the situations we face.

PRAYER

Sovereign God, help us to seek you in prayer before we seek answers to the problems we face.

60 DANIEL 9:4-10

DANIEL'S CONFESSION

Chapter 8 of Daniel draws quite heavily on Ezekiel, as well as having connections with other prophetic books like Isaiah and Zechariah. Chapter 9 explicitly refers to Jeremiah and seems to have many other links with that book. Its language is also similar to what we find in Deuteronomy.

Great and awesome God

Daniel's prayer starts with praise. He describes God as 'great' and 'awesome' (v. 4). The word 'great' was used often in the earlier chapters in relation to the Babylonian and Persian kings, and the word translated 'awesome' means 'to be feared'. As we noted earlier, the Hebrew word 'fear', just like the English word, can mean both 'be afraid of' and 'revere'. Daniel also describes the Lord as one who keeps 'covenant and steadfast love with those who love you and keep your commandments'. The concept of 'covenant' is a hugely important one in the Old Testament, describing the 'loyalty treaty' that the Lord establishes with God's people. The Lord is specifically one who enters into covenant with people who pledge allegiance to God. 'Steadfast love' is also a very important concept in the Old Testament. The word (*hesed*) is variously translated as 'loving kindness', 'mercy', 'loyalty', and so on, and in this case it describes the Lord's loving commitment to the Jews, specifically those 'who love [God] and keep [God's] commandments'. This is to say, the relationship between God and God's people is one of loving and loyal commitment on both sides. Verse 9 further points out that 'to the Lord our God belong mercy and forgiveness': even when God's people fail to maintain their side of the covenant, God still has mercy and demonstrates forgiveness.

The line 'great and awesome God, keeping covenant and steadfast love with those who love you and keep your commandments' occurs in almost identical form in Nehemiah 1:5, and seems also to draw on Deuteronomy 7:9. Indeed, the language here is very characteristic of the book of Deuteronomy. The 'name' of the Lord is also important in Deuteronomy (what's known as 'name theology'), and features in this chapter of Daniel, too (9:6, 15, 18, 19).

We have sinned

Following praise of God, the prayer turns to confession of sin. The word for 'sin' occurs often in this chapter, and there are five different expressions for sin in verse 5 alone: 'sinned', 'done wrong', 'acted wickedly', 'rebelled', and 'turned aside from your commandments and ordinances'. The sins of the Jews are greatly emphasized. This is picked up also in the sentence, 'We have not listened to your servants the prophets', which may refer to Jeremiah 25:4, 'And though the Lord persistently sent you all his servants the prophets, you have neither listened nor inclined your ears to hear', as well as a number of other passages in the Old Testament. It is notable, of course, that Daniel confesses on behalf of the Jews, even though he is not personally guilty of these sins.

Righteousness is on your side

Just as the sins of the Jews are emphasized, so also, by contrast, is the 'righteousness' of the Lord (v. 7). This is a key concept in the chapter (see vv. 7, 14, 16, 18, 24). The overall thrust of the prayer is that the relationship between God and the Jews has broken down because the Jews have sinned, while, as 9:14 states very starkly, 'the Lord our God is right [same basic word as 'righteousness' in Hebrew] in all that he has done.' The word 'righteousness' stands in contrast to the 'open shame' (v. 8, literally 'shame of face') of the Jews because of their sin. Sin is not usually a popular subject these days, and sometimes it seems that we try to do everything to explain away the things we do wrong, rather than taking responsibility for them, confessing them and turning from them. Daniel emphasizes the sins of the Jews and contrasts them with the righteousness of God, acknowledging that God is in the right (presumably in allowing the Jews to be taken off into exile in Babylon), while they are in the wrong.

REFLECTION

Do we as Christians focus enough on our sins? Are we sufficiently aware of our 'unrighteousness' compared to God's 'righteousness'? Of course, the other side of this issue is that some people are all too well aware of their sin and live under an inappropriate burden of guilt. The mercy and forgiveness of God are key: God does forgive us our sins if we confess them and turn from them.

The EXILE EXPLAINED

The previous section focused on Daniel's confession of the sins that the Jews (or, more accurately, the people of Judah before the fall of Jerusalem) had committed. This section focuses on the punishment that the Jews had endured as a result of their sins. Many of the expressions used here are found elsewhere in the Old Testament, particularly in Deuteronomy, Jeremiah and Nehemiah.

The calamity

The punishment is described three times using the same word, 'calamity' in the NRSV. This calamity is described as fulfilling 'the curse and the oath written in the law of Moses' (v. 11). Twice, these verses state that it was brought upon Jerusalem (and Judah) by God. The reasons for this are that 'all Israel has transgressed [God's] law and turned aside', they refused to obey God's voice, they sinned against God, and they did not entreat God by 'turning from [their] iniquities and reflecting on his fidelity' (v. 13). The calamity is described as 'so great' that it 'has never been done under the whole heaven' (v. 12), which is presumably exaggeration to emphasize that it is a very major disaster for the people of Judah. This calamity is the fall of Jerusalem, the sacking of the temple and the exiling of many people from Judah by the Babylonians in 587BC. This is the calamity that has been 'poured out upon us'—a phrase that probably draws on its use in Jeremiah, for example in 44:2–6: 'You yourselves have seen all the disaster [same word as 'calamity' in Daniel 9] that I have brought on Jerusalem and on all the towns of Judah... I persistently sent to you all my servants the prophets... But they did not listen... So my wrath and my anger were poured out and kindled in the towns of Judah and in the streets of Jerusalem; and they became a waste and a desolation' (see also Jeremiah 7:16–25).

The book of Lamentations describes graphically the extent of this calamity, chapter 1 repeatedly emphasizing that it resulted from the people's sins. (Note that Lamentations is traditionally assigned to Jeremiah.)

The curse and the oath

What has been 'poured out upon [them]' is specifically described as 'the curse and the oath written in the law of Moses'. Deuteronomy 28 relates the blessings that will accrue to Israel if they obey the law, but also the 'curses' that will befall them if they do not. The latter half of that chapter warns that they will be taken off into captivity in a foreign land, and describes repeatedly 'the desperate straits to which the enemy siege will reduce you in all your towns'. Deuteronomy 28:45 states that 'All these curses shall come upon you... because you did not obey the Lord your God', while Daniel 9:11 specifically observes that 'All Israel has transgressed your law and turned aside, refusing to obey your voice'. Therefore, the punishment was foretold and is well deserved.

The Lord our God is right

Daniel affirms that the punishment is deserved precisely because the Israelites have disobeyed: 'Indeed, the Lord our God is right in all that he has done; for we have disobeyed his voice' (v. 14). Daniel's words are close to those of Ezra in his prayer of confession: 'You have been just [same word as 'right'] in all that has come upon us, for you have dealt faithfully and we have acted wickedly; our kings, our officials, our priests, and our ancestors have not kept your law or heeded the commandments and the warnings that you gave them' (Nehemiah 9:33–34).

Daniel reflects back on the calamity that was the exile and, drawing on 'scripture', concludes that the Jews are only suffering what Moses and Jeremiah (among others) warned about. It is their just punishment for disobeying what God had commanded in the law. We can conclude from this that there may be severe consequences when we disobey what God has commanded. Whether or not we believe that today God will 'punish' individuals, communities or even whole nations (and people hold very different views on this matter), I think it is right to conclude that if we stray from God's will, people will suffer, sometimes very severely, as a result.

REFLECTION

Can you think of ways in which our disobedience of God's laws— as individuals, communities and nations—causes people to suffer?

HEAR, FORGIVE, LISTEN, ACT

Daniel's prayer has moved from praise of God, to confession, to an explanation of why the exile had occurred. It now draws to its conclusion with specific petitions being made to God. No requests were made in the previous eleven verses of the prayer. Now petitions are dotted throughout verses 16–19, but they come to a dramatic climax in the final verse: 'O Lord, hear; O Lord, forgive; O Lord, listen and act and do not delay!'

This section falls into two halves, both starting with the same word, 'and now' (one word in Hebrew). Verses 15 and 16 look back to the foundational event of the exodus of the Israelites from Egypt, and call on the God who displayed righteousness there to do similarly in the current situation. Verses 17 and 18 then plead with God to hear Daniel's prayer, primarily on the grounds of God's own reputation. Verse 19 is the climactic conclusion to the whole prayer.

Name theology

We noted earlier that names were very important in the world of the ancient Near East. Name and reputation are very closely associated, and the importance of maintaining God's 'name' or 'reputation' is a key element especially in Deuteronomy and in Ezekiel. Twice in this passage from Daniel, reference is made to 'the city that bears your name'—that is, Jerusalem—and, indeed, Jerusalem is specifically mentioned twice. 'Your holy mountain' refers to Zion, where Jerusalem was built. Moreover, the temple is referred to as 'your desolated sanctuary' (v. 17). Surely the Lord's name/reputation must suffer when the city and temple that bear his name lie in ruins? Daniel also reflects back to the foundational event of the exodus, noting how it had been key in establishing the Lord's reputation and making his name known among the nations. He calls on the Lord to act on Israel's behalf again, to repeat the 'righteous acts' of the past by delivering 'your people [who] bear your name', because 'your people have become a disgrace among all our neighbours' (v. 16). Effectively, Daniel's plea is that although the Israelites 'have sinned' and 'have done wickedly', nonetheless God, in great mercy, should turn away from (justifiable) anger and wrath so that the Lord's reputation might be maintained among the nations. Daniel says to God twice in these verses that the Lord should act 'for your own sake'.

The petitions

At the end of the prayer, the petitions come pouring out. There are three occurrences of 'hear' in verses 17–19 that are very emphatic. Daniel's first petition is that God will hear him. The next request is for 'forgiveness' or 'pardon'. He appeals for forgiveness on the basis of God's righteousness and great mercy and with repeated reference to God's reputation. Finally, 'listen' means something like 'give attention to', which might be seen as the step between 'hearing' and 'acting': hear; then give attention to; then act. 'Act' clearly means 'do something about it!' Daniel is looking for something to change, specifically that the desolation of Jerusalem be reversed—and not sometime in the future, but soon: 'Do not delay!' For all his forthrightness, however, Daniel seems to have paid careful attention to such scriptures as Ezekiel 20, and concludes by reiterating that his requests are all to the end that God's reputation might be maintained: 'For your own sake, O my God, because your city and your people bear your name!'

Daniel's prayer provides a wonderful model for us to draw on. It starts by praising God, making specific reference to how the Lord is portrayed in the scriptures. It then offers heartfelt confession, again drawing on scripture and noting specific ways in which the people have sinned. Next it reflects on the particular situation that has called forth the prayer, relating this too to the scriptures. And finally it turns to petition—and these are no feeble, tentative requests, but full-blooded, confident pleadings which, in clear and unambiguous language, call on God to hear, forgive, listen and act quickly, and all for the sake of God's good name!

REFLECTION

As you reflect back on this prayer, think about how your own prayers, and the prayers you hear in church and perhaps elsewhere, compare.

63

DANIEL 9:20–23

WHILE I WAS PRAYING...

Daniel's prayer comes to an end in 9:19, but verse 20 emphasizes, and verse 21 reiterates, that God's response comes while Daniel is still speaking. Whether this indicates that Daniel's prayer was interrupted by Gabriel's arrival, or whether Gabriel arrived the very instant that Daniel's prayer finished, is not clear. Either way, the point is clearly made that, following Daniel's petitions, God's response is immediate. Verse 23, though, indicates that the response was even quicker than this: 'At the beginning of your supplications a word went out.'

In conclusion

Verse 20 acts as a summary of Daniel's prayer and picks up on 9:3–4. It draws the prayer section of the chapter to a close, specifically highlighting words used in earlier verses and indicating the main focus of Daniel's supplications—that is, Mount Zion, the city of Jerusalem built upon it, and the temple built within Jerusalem. Some commentators have rightly pointed out that the narrative would run smoothly if verses 4–20 were omitted altogether and the text ran straight on from verse 3 to verse 21. This is true, and it is possible that the prayer was added later. Nonetheless, it now plays a very important role in the chapter and is a highly significant part of the text as we have it.

A word went out

Verses 20 and 21 indicate the immediacy of God's response to Daniel's prayer, but verse 23 states that actually God responded as soon as Daniel started to pray. This seems to imply that it was not so much what Daniel prayed as the fact that he did pray that was important. It's almost as if God was waiting for Daniel to pray so that he could act, and as soon as the prayer started, God's plan swung into action. Some commentators have read this to imply that the content of Daniel's prayer did not matter; God had determined ahead of time what was going to happen, and the words Daniel said were irrelevant. As Lucas says, however, 'This is too rationalistic a reading', adding that it 'arises partly because scholars ignore the prayer since they doubt whether it is an integral part of the chapter'. Rather, Lucas argues, 'it is evidence of God's eagerness to listen and respond' (p. 252).

This passage raises important questions about our theology of prayer. We should bear in mind what the psalmist says to God in Psalm 139:2, 4: 'You discern my thoughts from far away', and 'Even before a word is on my tongue, O Lord, you know it completely'. Moreover, in Isaiah 65:24 the Lord states, 'Before they call I will answer, while they are yet speaking I will hear.' The implications seem to be that God knows what we will pray before we say the words, but God does, at times at least, wait for us to pray before acting. Also, God hears our prayers, and God does, at times at least, act immediately (if not sooner!) in response to our prayers, even if the answer is not quite what we were looking for.

The man Gabriel

We were introduced to Gabriel in 8:15–17. There he was described as 'having the appearance of a man', but here he is simply described as 'the man Gabriel' (v. 21). It may be that this is a shorthand way of saying the same thing, and certainly the way he is described indicates that he is no mere human. In fact, his coming 'in swift flight' may indicate that angels (or celestial 'messengers'), like seraphim (Isaiah 6:2) and cherubim (Exodus 25:20), have wings, although I suspect that this is a metaphorical way of speaking. The fact that Gabriel is described as the one 'whom I had seen before in a vision' (v. 21) establishes a clear link between chapters 8 and 9, and we might note that just as in chapter 8 his task was to 'help this man understand the vision', here, too, he states, 'I have now come out to give you wisdom and understanding' (v. 22). Notice also that he tells Daniel that he is 'greatly beloved' (v. 23); such reassurance is a key aspect of how God relates to Daniel through his messenger.

REFLECTION

In Daniel's case, it appears that the prayer of one individual on behalf of a sinful nation did elicit a specific and immediate response from God. How does this tie in with your understanding and experience of prayer?

The SEVENTY WEEKS EXPLAINED

This passage has generated more controversy than just about any other in Daniel. In very general terms, interpretation falls into two camps. First, there are those who read the passage christologically, viewing it as focusing on Jesus, and second, there are others who read the passage in light of the events related to Antiochus IV Epiphanes in the second century BC. Even within these two camps, however, there are many variations. Walton's book, *Chronological and Background Charts of the Old Testament* (p. 106), summarizes various positions helpfully, although it is not exhaustive.

The seventy weeks

The 'seventy years' of Jeremiah's prophecy are here reinterpreted as 'seventy sevens' (the Hebrew word for 'week' is 'seven'), which is usually taken to mean 490 years. This probably relates to the warning in Leviticus 26:18: 'if in spite of this you will not obey me, I will continue to punish you sevenfold for your sins', a warning repeated in 26:21, 24 and 28—hence greatly emphasized. It might be seen as 'the land [making] up for its sabbaths' (2 Chronicles 36:18–21, which also refers to 'the word of the Lord by the mouth of Jeremiah').

The seventy 'sevens' or 'weeks' are further divided into seven weeks, 62 weeks, and a final week divided into two halves. All sorts of dates have been proposed in order to establish precisely when these 490 years were, and which events fell at the end of the seventh, 62nd and 70th 'weeks'. A number of commentators work through the various options. In the end, none of the arguments for precise dating fits precisely, and I believe that those commentators (of whom there are an increasing number) are correct who maintain that the numbers are meant symbolically rather than in a precise literal sense. That still leaves the question of whether the passage relates to Jesus or to Antiochus, and even those who agree that the numbers are symbolic are not agreed on this question. My best guess (along with the vast majority of scholars) is that when the passage was written, it had in view the events associated with Antiochus IV Epiphanes in the second century BC. This would mean that the first seven 'weeks' indicate (roughly) the period of the Babylonian exile; the 62 weeks are the period running from the Persian king Cyrus (who overthrew the Babylonian empire in around 539BC and allowed Jews to return to Judah) to Antiochus; and the final week relates to the events in Jerusalem in the 160s BC, including the half week when Antiochus desecrated the temple and prohibited Jewish worship, and leading up to the restoration of the temple in 164BC. Even if that view is correct, however, the whole passage, while based on the events in the second century BC, can be seen as having relevance beyond that period, and being further 'fulfilled' in the life, death, resurrection and second coming of Jesus.

Interpretation

This passage, perhaps more than any other in Daniel, raises questions about how we interpret the Old Testament in light of the New Testament. For most of Christian history, these verses have been understood to refer to Jesus, but many scholars and others today would argue that they are actually about events known to the writer, which culminated in the second century BC. I have argued (along with other scholars) that this material does relate to the second century BC and derives from that time, but that its meaning is not exhausted by those events. Thus it is valid to relate the passage further to Jesus' life, death, resurrection and second coming.

REFLECTION

What are the implications of this approach for your reading of other parts of the Bible?

The SIX BLESSINGS

Lederach (p. 213) helpfully picks out six 'blessings' in verse 24. It should be noted that while these blessings may well have wider relevance, in the second-century context they specifically relate to the Jews and to Jerusalem: 'your people and your holy city'.

Dealing with sin

The first three blessings are as follows.

1) To finish transgression. This may refer back to 'the transgression that desolates' in 8:13, which might also relate to the 'abomination that desolates' in 9:27. Alternatively, 'transgression' could be synonymous with 'sin' and 'iniquity'. Whatever precisely is meant, however, the promise here is that it will come to an end.

2) To put an end to sin. The word for sin occurs only in chapter 9 in Daniel, but here it occurs often: in 9:5, 8, 11 and 15, Daniel confesses, 'we have sinned'; in 9:16, he notes God's 'anger and wrath... because of our sins'; and in 9:20, he confesses his own sins and the sins of his people. This blessing seems to be a specific response to Daniel's confession.

3) To atone for iniquity. 'Iniquity' appears twice earlier in the chapter (and nowhere else in the book). In 9:13, Daniel acknowledges that 'we did not entreat the favour of the Lord our God, turning from our iniquities', while in 9:16 he refers to God's 'anger and wrath... because of our sins and the iniquities of our ancestors', as a result of which 'Jerusalem and [God's] people have become a disgrace among all our neighbours'. 'Atoning' for (or 'covering over') iniquities does not occur elsewhere in Daniel, but is a theme through much of the Old Testament (especially in Leviticus and Numbers). It is also, of course, a key theme in the New Testament.

Taken together, these three blessings indicate that at the end of the 'seventy weeks', God will act decisively to deal with past sin.

Righteousness, sealing and anointing

The remaining three blessings are as follows.

4) To bring in everlasting righteousness. This picks up on the key theme of God's righteousness in Daniel's prayer. 'Righteousness is on your side,' declares 9:7; 'the Lord our God is right in all that he has done,' states 9:14, and Daniel petitions God to turn away anger and wrath in view of all God's 'righteous acts' in 9:16. The emphasis is upon God's righteousness, which alone can overcome people's sinfulness, and the promise here is that everlasting righteousness will be established when God deals with people's sins.

5) To seal both vision and prophet. There is some dispute about the meaning of this phrase. Does it imply that the vision will be 'sealed up' and effectively kept secret until that time in the future (from the perspective of the sixth-century Daniel) when these events will come to pass (see 8:26; 12:4, 9)? Or does it indicate that God's 'seal of approval' will be stamped upon both the vision and the prophet? Because the prophet appears here, and the sentence immediately goes on to refer to the anointing of 'a most holy place' (in fulfilment of the vision), the latter seems more likely. That is to say, God is affirming that the things promised here will come to pass.

6) To anoint a most holy place. Anointing indicates God's blessing. As noted earlier, the primary focus of these verses is Jerusalem and the temple. The second-century fulfilment of the blessings promised here is the rededication of the temple, which symbolized God's presence among his people and indicated his willingness to forgive them. When the temple is once again anointed, the relationship between God and the Jews will be restored. It should be noted, though, that the phrase translated 'a most holy place' is literally 'holy of holies', which in Hebrew is an idiom meaning 'the most holy thing' or 'one'. While, in its second-century context, this seems clearly to refer to the temple, that need not exhaust its possible meanings.

REFLECTION

The blessings are a specific response to Daniel's petitions. Verse 24 makes it clear that his prayer has been heard, that the sins he confessed on behalf of the Jews have been dealt with, and that God has seen the 'desolations' and promises to 'anoint' the 'desolated sanctuary'. Hence, in this chapter we find specific answers to the specific requests Daniel presented in prayer.

66 DANIEL 9:24–27 (III)

LOOKING FORWARD *to* JESUS?

There are two further important points from this passage, to which we should devote some attention. The first is the use of the word 'anoint', in the sense of the anointing of 'a most holy place' (the temple in Jerusalem) in verse 24, and in the terms 'an anointed prince' (v. 25) and 'an anointed one' (v. 26). These two terms have often been taken as references to Jesus as the 'Messiah'. The second important point is the use of the word 'desolate', which is used of general 'desolations' in verse 26, and in the terms 'an abomination that desolates' and 'the desolator' in verse 27. 'The desolator' has often been taken as a reference to an end-time 'antichrist' (= anti-Messiah).

The anointed ones

The word 'anointed' is literally in Hebrew 'Messiah' (pronounced *mashiach*), which is the word 'Christ' (*christos* in Greek) in the New Testament. The Christian (and later Jewish) concept of a particular individual as Messiah doesn't occur explicitly in the Old Testament, and should not be read here. The text refers simply to 'an anointed prince' and 'an anointed one', and readers and interpreters are left to work out who is being referred to. Probably, the people in mind are two high priests: the sixth-century high priest Joshua (or Jeshua), referred to in Ezra, Nehemiah, Haggai and Zechariah alongside the governor Zerubbabel at the time of the rebuilding of the temple; and the second-century high priest Onias III, who was deposed by Antiochus in 171BC. A contrast is being drawn between the leader approved by God, the 'anointed prince' Joshua (v. 25), and the one who usurps authority, the 'prince' (same word in Hebrew) Antiochus, who 'shall destroy the city and the sanctuary' (v. 26) that Joshua helped to rebuild some three and a half centuries earlier.

The desolator

Emphasis is placed at the end of this passage on 'desolations': in general, 'desolations' are decreed, an 'abomination that desolates' (v. 27) will be set up, but eventually the decreed end will come upon the 'desolator'. Earlier in the chapter we read of 'your desolated sanctuary' (9:17) and God was called to 'look at our desolation' (9:18). In chapter 8 we read of the 'transgression that makes desolate' (8:13). In the second-century context, the 'desolations' refer to what Antiochus did in Jerusalem: the 'abomination that desolates' (here and again in 11:31 and 12:11) refers to the setting up of an altar to Zeus (on which pigs were sacrificed) in the temple, where Jewish sacrifices should have been offered; and the 'desolator' is Antiochus himself. But the most significant thing here is that, at the very end of the chapter, it is declared that this desolator, Antiochus IV Epiphanes, the greatest threat facing the Jews at the time, has his end decreed—and it will come about soon.

As stated previously, it is my view that what we are reading about in these verses are people, things and events in Jewish history before the time of Christ—mostly in the second century BC. However, the blessings we considered in the previous section were clearly not fulfilled in a literal sense in the second century. God does seem to have set his 'seal of approval' both on Daniel's vision and on Daniel himself as a prophet. The temple, as 'a most holy place', was 'anointed' when Judas Maccabee rededicated it in 164BC. But, while specific transgression may have been 'finished', specific sins and iniquities ended and atoned for, and God's righteousness re-established in a sense, nonetheless transgression, sin, iniquity and unrighteousness continue. Christians believe that Jesus brought about a final completion of transgression, a real end to sin and a once-for-all atonement for iniquity; moreover, in him everlasting righteousness is achieved and imputed to those who believe in him by faith. In addition, while the 'anointed' ones ('messiahs') probably relate to specific individuals in Jewish history, in Jesus we find a Messiah like no other, who was 'cut off' by his death on the cross. I would argue, therefore, that we can read the passage in light of its second-century setting, but still find that its meaning is not exhausted by such a reading.

REFLECTION

In what ways do you think this passage might relate to Jesus? Note that 1 John 1:5–10 relates well to Daniel 9, particularly the words, 'the blood of Jesus his Son cleanses us from all sin… If we confess our sins, he who is faithful and just [or 'righteous'] will forgive us our sins and cleanse us from all unrighteousness'.

The REVEALED WORD

The final section of the book consists of chapters 10—12. The vision proper is to be found in 11:2—12:4, while 10:1—11:1 and 12:5–13 serve as the introduction and conclusion to the section.

We noted earlier that the book of Daniel draws on material from elsewhere in the Old Testament and relates it to events late in the Babylonian exile and in the following centuries, right up to the second century BC. Goldingay describes this as 'the anthologizing of Scripture'. He states that it 'becomes central in chaps. 10—12', and 'it enables the seer to develop a systematic interpretation of past, present, and future as a whole that will enable his people to live with these' (p. 285). This is very significant because Goldingay, along with many other scholars, reads most of the material in this section as 'quasi-prediction' rather than genuine 'predictive' prophecy. It is, according to Goldingay, written some time around 165BC and, in a style similar to other literature of the time, it reflects back on past history, casting it as a vision seen in the sixth century by Daniel but interpreting these events in light of scripture. Thus, the events in 11:2–39 correlate very well with what we know from elsewhere of the history of the period. The events in 11:40—12:3 do not, however, and Goldingay, along with many others, takes this latter section as prophecy that genuinely looks to the future from the perspective of the writer. He states that it is 'the quasi-predictions' ability to make sense of the past by relating it in the light of Scripture that implies grounds for trusting the actual prophecy's portrait of what the future will bring, painted in the light of the same Scripture' (p. 285). Hence, what is of most concern here is not the accuracy of Daniel's 'predic-tions', but rather the ability of the writer to interpret past, present and future events in light of existing scripture. Goldingay's approach here is the most helpful way to view the vision.

The third year of King Cyrus

Like other chapters, chapter 10 begins with a time reference, which, in this case, indicates that the Babylonian exile is over, Cyrus the Persian has issued his edict permitting Jews to return to their land, and Jeremiah's 'seventy years' have come to an end. However, one of the main messages of Daniel is that 'exile' did not, in fact, end when Babylonian dominance ceased, but actually continued right up to the second century BC. It may be that the use of Daniel's captive name here, Belteshazzar, is an indication of continuing exile.

A word

The word for 'word' is repeated three times in verse 1, and this picks up on its use in chapter 9. In 9:2 Daniel was reading 'the word of the Lord according to the prophet Jeremiah', which indicates that the Lord's word was to be found in scripture. Here (as also in 9:23), the word comes through a vision. This word is 'revealed' to Daniel, it is 'true', and Daniel 'understood the word' because he received 'understanding in the vision'. 'Words' are important in chapters 10 and 12 of Daniel (and the verb 'to speak' in these chapters is from the same Hebrew root).

Apocalyptic literature

This section of Daniel displays more elements of what is termed 'apocalyptic literature' than we find in other parts of the book (or, indeed, than we find elsewhere in the Old Testament). Apocalyptic literature is markedly different from most other Old Testament prophecy—although there are some examples of apocalyptic material in Isaiah, Joel, Zechariah and perhaps Ezekiel—and needs to be read differently from other Old Testament material if the reader is to understand it as the author intended. Thus, what Goldingay describes as 'quasi-prophecy' is typical of apocalyptic material and occurs also in other ancient material from Mesopotamia, Egypt and Greece. The writer, then, was employing a recognized strategy for conveying God's 'word' to the faithful Jews of the second century BC, and not trying to deceive people into believing that these were actually the words of a sixth-century prophet called Daniel.

PRAYER

Sovereign God, thank you for revealing your word to us. Help us to understand your word and to know its truth for us.

A MAN CLOTHED IN LINEN

In Daniel 7:10 we were introduced to the 'ten thousand times ten thousand' who 'stood attending' God. It was presumably one of these 'attendants' whom Daniel then approached 'to ask him the truth concerning all this', and the attendant 'said that he would disclose... the interpretation of the matter' (7:16). The attendant appeared to be a celestial being, an angel. In chapter 8, the angel Gabriel, who was described as 'having the appearance of a man' (8:15), provided Daniel with the interpretation of his vision. In chapter 9, Gabriel, now described simply as 'the man Gabriel', appeared again to give Daniel understanding and to convey a vision to him. Now in chapter 10 we meet 'a man clothed in linen' (v. 5) who also comes to Daniel to speak a 'word' (from God) to him—presumably the word described in 10:1 as 'revealed' and 'true', and about which Daniel gained understanding in his vision.

Mourning for three weeks

In 9:3, Daniel sought God by 'prayer and supplication with fasting and sackcloth and ashes'. Fasting, sackcloth and ashes were used in mourning, and here in chapter 10 we are specifically told that Daniel 'had been mourning for three weeks' (v. 2). He had also been fasting, because 'no rich food, no meat or wine had entered [his] mouth... for the full three weeks' (v. 3). This suggests that at other times Daniel did eat rich food and meat and drink wine, which means that his refusal to eat 'the royal rations of food and wine', recorded in chapter 1, was for a limited period only. Daniel's mourning and fasting indicate the seriousness with which he undertook his search for understanding of what God was doing in the situation in which Daniel found himself. We might recall Nehemiah's response to news about the state of Jerusalem: 'When I heard these words I sat down and wept, and mourned for days, fasting and praying before the God of heaven' (Nehemiah 1:4).

'The 24th day of the first month'

'The first month' (v. 4) is Nisan (March/April), and from the 15th to the 21st day of that month the major Jewish festivals of Passover and

Unleavened Bread were celebrated. This means that Daniel fasted right through a period that was normally a time of great celebration for Jews. In the second-century context, however, Antiochus had desecrated the temple and forbidden observation of the Jewish festivals, and 1 Maccabees states that the feasts of the Jews were turned into mourning.

Gabriel

The 'man clothed in linen' is probably the same being that will be referred to in 10:16 and 18 as 'one in human form'. He appears again in 12:6–7, where he is joined by 'two others' (the occurrences of the phrase 'man clothed in linen' at either end of this section may function as an *inclusio*, marking its beginning and end). It seems likely that all these descriptions refer to Gabriel. What is perhaps most noteworthy is that the description of Gabriel here seems to draw heavily on the book of Ezekiel, especially as the expression 'man clothed in linen' occurs elsewhere in the Old Testament only in the vision described in Ezekiel 9 and 10 (9:2, 3, 11; 10:2, 6, 7). In these chapters the 'man clothed in linen' has a role that fits very well with Gabriel's role in Daniel. Moreover, verse 4 of our passage is similar to the opening verse of Ezekiel, and just about every detail concerning the 'man clothed in linen' in verses 5–6 finds its parallel in the first chapter of Ezekiel (especially verses 7, 13, 16, 24, 27).

Clearly, Daniel takes very seriously the task of trying to understand how God was involved in the events of his day. He not only mourned and fasted, but he did this during one of the biggest Jewish festivals of the year—a bit like us mourning and fasting over the Christmas period. Then, God responds to Daniel by sending a divine messenger to help him understand, and that understanding involves the word of God communicated through a vision.

REFLECTION

How seriously do we take the task of trying to understand
how God is involved in the events of our day? Do we really
mourn the state of our nation and strive to understand
what God's word is for our situation?

DANIEL'S DAMASCUS ROAD?

In this short section, Daniel describes his response to the vision, and it turns out to be very similar to his response to earlier visions recorded in 4:19; 7:15, 28 and 8:27. It seems that this kind of encounter with the divine realm is no picnic!

I alone saw the vision

The text emphasizes that Daniel alone saw the vision, and this emphasis is achieved by a grammatically redundant repetition of 'I', repetition of the words 'alone' and 'was left', and the use twice of the words, '*I* saw the vision', contrasted with one occurrence of '*they* did not see the vision'. This indicates both that the experience was one that Daniel had to endure completely alone and also that it had a dramatic impact upon him. The dramatic impact is conveyed by the repetition of Daniel's strength leaving him, by the emphasis at the end of the passage on Daniel being face-down on the ground, and the very strong clause that might be rendered 'my vigour turned against me to ruin' (v. 8).

Like Paul's Damascus road vision?

This all sounds rather reminiscent of the experience of Saul (later the apostle Paul) on the road to Damascus (Acts 22:6–9):

> About noon a great light from heaven suddenly shone about me. I fell to the ground and heard a voice saying to me, 'Saul, Saul, why are you persecuting me?' I answered, 'Who are you, Lord?' Then he said to me, 'I am Jesus of Nazareth whom you are persecuting.' Now those who were with me saw the light but did not hear the voice of the one who was speaking to me.

Here, too, Saul had to endure his experience alone, although there were other people with him, and his encounter with the divine also had a dramatic impact upon him.

Similarities to other scriptures

The description of 'one like the Son of Man' in Revelation 1, which takes some of its imagery from Daniel 7, also draws upon Daniel 10 in its description of a being who was 'clothed with a long robe', whose eyes were 'like a flame of fire', whose feet were 'like burnished bronze' and whose voice was 'like the sound of many waters'. John says, 'When I saw him, I fell at his feet as though dead' (Revelation 1:13–15, 17), much as Daniel here 'fell into a trance, face to the ground' (v. 9).

But while Revelation draws on Daniel for its imagery, it may be that Daniel here again draws on Ezekiel 1, because after describing 'something that seemed like a human form', using language that bears marked similarities to Daniel 10:4–6, Ezekiel states, 'When I saw it, I fell on my face, and I heard the voice of someone speaking' (Ezekiel 1:28). Ezekiel then hears words spoken to him which presumably come from God—just as Daniel does later in chapter 10.

The role of a prophet

In the Christian Bible, the book of Daniel is found among the prophets (but not in the Jewish Bible, where it is one of the 'Writings'). In some ways, Daniel is quite unlike the other prophets, although, as we have seen, the book draws extensively on Isaiah, Jeremiah and Ezekiel in particular. Daniel as an individual, however, shares many things in common with the historical prophets, such as the eighth-century Isaiah and the seventh- to sixth-century Jeremiah and Ezekiel. One of these similarities is that at times he had to plough a rather lonely furrow. Although Christianity (and Judaism, too) is essentially a community religion rather than an individual one, life can at times be very lonely for those whom God calls specifically to hear and proclaim God's prophetic word. The role of a prophet (or of a prophetic preacher or evangelist or writer) can be very hard as they struggle with what God reveals to them, and sometimes carry that burden, at least to some extent, alone. Genuine prophetic insight into, for example, the state of our nation can have a dramatic impact on the 'prophet', and may well leave that person deeply troubled and feeling very alone.

REFLECTION

Is this something you have ever experienced? How do you think you might cope if you did? How might you be able to support others who have this 'gift'?

YOUR WORDS HAVE BEEN HEARD

This section, along with some details from earlier in the chapter, is remarkably similar to those passages in chapters 8 (8:15–19) and 9 (9:21–23) which describe the appearance of Gabriel. Thus, once again, when Daniel seeks understanding of God's 'word', Gabriel comes to give him understanding. Furthermore, the parallels do not just occur across these three chapters; emphasis is also achieved by repetition within chapter 10 itself. Thus, the same points are made in both 10:8–14 and 10:15–21.

A hand touched me

In 8:18, as in 10:9, Daniel fell to the ground in a trance, and was roused by Gabriel's 'touch' (v. 10). (The 'touch' of Gabriel is also mentioned in 9:21, although the word is not apparent in English.) The same thing happens again later in chapter 10, where 'Again one in human form touched me and strengthened me' (10:18). The 'touching' in 10:16 is particularly noteworthy, because it again links this chapter with Isaiah (see 6:7) and Jeremiah (see 1:9): 'Then one in human form touched my lips, and I opened my mouth to speak.'

Words and speaking

'Words' are again very important in this section, which correlates with the significance of Gabriel's touch here and in 10:16 and 18. Verses 11 and 12 start with an identical phrase in Hebrew: 'He said to me'. When the NRSV refers to 'speaking' in verse 11, a different word is used, which comes from the same root as the Hebrew for 'word'. Hence, words from this root occur six times in the two verses. The four occurrences in verse 11—'the *words* that I am going to *speak* to you' and 'while he was *speaking* this *word* to me'—all refer to Gabriel's words. This emphasizes the great importance of these words: Daniel is to 'pay attention to' (literally 'understand') them as of first importance. The words that Gabriel speaks, however, come in response to Daniel's own words. Thus it may well be that here, as in chapter 9, God's response is elicited by Daniel's words in prayer, and again God's response is immediate ('from the first day…', v. 12), although in this instance Gabriel was detained by 'the prince of the kingdom of Persia' (v. 13).

Michael and the prince of Persia

It looks as though the concept here is one that was widespread in the ancient Near East: the idea of a divine council consisting of angels or gods representing all the nations. Here 'the prince of the kingdom of Persia' seems to be the patron angel of Persia, who is battling with Michael, the patron angel of the Jews (note that Michael is described as 'your prince' in 10:21 and 'the protector of your people' in 12:1). In verses 2 and 3 of chapter 10 we were twice told that Daniel mourned for three weeks, and here the reason is given for the delay between the first day, when God heard Daniel's words, and 21 days later when Gabriel eventually appears: he and Michael were engaged in a battle with the Persian patron angel.

A delayed response

A key point to note here is that God does respond to the words we utter to him, but that it may take time for us to see that response because of circumstances about which we can know nothing. Moreover, what God says in response may be very difficult for us to understand and may require insight that God himself grants, perhaps through some divine medium, whether that be a celestial messenger or the Holy Spirit. Daniel is assured by Gabriel that he need not fear. Daniel has sought God with his mind ('you set your mind to gain understanding'), by his actions ('to humble yourself before your God') and through his speech ('your words have been heard'), and God has responded. If we seek God with our minds, actions and speech (and we might note that Daniel's emotions are involved here, too), he will respond to us, even though it may take some time for us to perceive that response.

PRAYER

Sovereign God, may we seek you with our minds,
by our actions and through our speech, and learn to wait
patiently for your response.

DO NOT FEAR, GREATLY BELOVED!

In the previous section, Daniel was called 'greatly beloved' and was told, 'Do not fear.' These two phrases are brought together at the centre of this passage where Gabriel says, 'Do not fear, greatly beloved' (v. 19), then goes on to assure Daniel, 'You are safe' (the actual words are 'peace [*shalom*] to you'). In fact, we noted in the previous section that this passage reiterates much that appeared in the earlier verses, although here the emphasis is different. The main emphasis follows the words 'you are safe', where the NRSV translates, 'Be strong and courageous!' but the Hebrew repeats the same word twice: 'Be strong and be strong!'

Words and touch

Again, words for 'word' and 'speak' are very important. These terms are used much more in this section and the previous one than anywhere else in Daniel. The word with which both 10:11 and 10:12 start ('he said') is used four times in this passage as well. As we noted in the previous section, here too Gabriel's touch is important. In the first instance, it is Daniel's lips that are touched (v. 16), which ties in with the emphasis on words and speaking. On the second occasion when Daniel is touched, it is to 'strengthen' him (v. 18), and we will pick up on this below.

Michael and the prince of Persia again

Michael and the prince of Persia appear here again, but this time they are joined by 'the prince of Greece' (v. 20). The Persian empire fell to the Greeks around 333BC, just over 200 years after the fall of the Babylonian empire. As the Jews suffered under first the Persians and then the Greeks, so, it seems, Michael as the patron angel of the Jews ('your prince') contended first with the Persians and then with the Greeks ('these princes', v. 21).

One in human form

The word for 'form' in verse 16 is the same word as 'likeness' in Genesis 1:26: 'Then God said, "Let us make humankind in our image, according to our likeness."' In the NRSV the identical phrase, 'one in human form', is used in Daniel 10:18, but the word for 'form' is different in Hebrew and might better be rendered 'appearance'. The exact phrase used here occurs elsewhere only in Ezekiel 1:26, a verse that also uses the word 'likeness' twice. Hence, further links are established between Daniel and Ezekiel, and the humanlike appearance of Gabriel is emphasized again.

Strengthening

The key theme of 'strengthening' in this passage picks up on the references in 10:8 to Daniel's strength leaving him because of the vision he saw. Two different words for 'strength' are used, although this is not apparent in the NRSV. The repeated references to Daniel losing his strength in 10:8, 16 and 17 use one word, while the references to Daniel being strengthened by Gabriel's touch in verse 18 and twice in verse 19 use another word. In Hebrew, this word occurs once in verse 18, four times in verse 19, once in verse 20 and once in 11:1. Clearly, Gabriel's strengthening of Daniel is a key element in these few verses.

This passage highlights the importance of the words God speaks, whether they come through a divine or perhaps human messenger, or through the words of scripture (recalling Daniel's constant allusions to other parts of the Old Testament). The main point, however, is the 'strengthening' that God provides (here through the angel Gabriel) to enable Daniel to cope with the message God has for him. When God calls us to a task, he does provide the strength with which to do it. Thus, as God says to the exiles in Isaiah 41:10, 'Do not fear, for I am with you, do not be afraid, for I am your God; I will strengthen you, I will help you, I will uphold you with my victorious right hand.' That strength may come by supernatural means, or it may come from a human messenger whom God sends to help us.

PRAYER

Sovereign God, may we know you strengthening us
for the tasks to which you call us.

The PERSIAN & GREEK EMPIRES

This section is the beginning of Gabriel's description of history (in 11:2–45), starting with the Persian empire, then focusing on the Greek empire (particularly the Seleucid and Ptolemaic kingdoms), before concluding with events associated with Antiochus IV Epiphanes (a Seleucid king). It presents an accurate portrayal of this history, most of the details of which can be confirmed from elsewhere. This is generally agreed among scholars, and, for readers who are interested, Goldingay (pp. 295–6) has a helpful diagram showing how these verses tie in with the history of the period.

Three more kings and a fourth

There is some debate about just who the 'three more kings' and 'the fourth' who 'shall be far richer than all of them' might be (v. 2). There were 13 kings who ruled over the Persian empire before it fell to the Greeks, although only four of them are mentioned in the Old Testament: Cyrus, Darius, Xerxes (or Ahasuerus) and Artaxerxes (see Ezra 4:5–7). These might be the four intended, but Artaxerxes doesn't fit the description of the fourth king. The king who best fits that description is Xerxes I (or Ahasuerus), who was very wealthy and did invade Greece (although he was then defeated). Xerxes I was the fifth Persian king, but he was the fourth after Cyrus, so if the perspective was looking forward from Daniel's time it might refer to the four consecutive kings Cambyses (Cyrus's successor), Smerdis, Darius I and Xerxes I. This, however, would mean leaving a gap of over a century before the events of verse 3, which reads as though it should follow straight on. An alternative explanation, and the one I think most likely, is that verse 2 does not refer to specific kings, but is using a rhetorical device to refer to all the Persian kings. We find this device, known as a 'graduated numerical saying', elsewhere in the Old Testament, where a number is followed by the next number up. Thus, for example, Amos 1 and 2 repeatedly mention 'For three transgressions… and for four', and Proverbs 30 also contains a series that follows the pattern 'three things… four'. The particular 'three' and 'four' are not, in themselves, greatly significant, but are representative examples.

The warrior king

There is general agreement that the 'warrior king' (v. 3) refers to Alexander the Great. Thus, the 'three' and 'fourth' Persian kings, representing the whole Persian empire, fell to the warrior king Alexander the Great. What is most notable about this warrior king is that he will 'take action as he pleases'. Exactly the same thing (in Hebrew) is said about the ram (representing Persia) in Daniel's vision in chapter 8, which 'did as it pleased' (8:4), about Antiochus III who 'shall take the actions he pleases' (11:16) and of Antiochus IV who also 'shall act as he pleases' (11:36). An important theme in this vision, then, is that these powerful kings act as they want, presumably imagining that their power gives them the right to do so.

The four winds of heaven

Alexander's reign did not last long. He died of a fever in 323BC, aged only 33. The empire did not then pass on to one of his sons ('not to his posterity', v. 4), but was divided among four of his generals. These four were known as 'the Diadochoi' (successors), and they may be what is meant by 'the four winds of heaven'; alternatively, 'four' may be used symbolically, simply to indicate that the great empire established by Alexander did not continue beyond his death but was split up.

From the perspective of the Jews, it must have seemed as though these great empires wielded tremendous power, against which they had no hope of standing. It must have appeared at times as though the kings acted as they pleased, with no regard for the God of the Jews, yet were very successful. Where, then, was the evidence of God's power? One of the main messages of Daniel is that, despite appearances, God is ultimately in control, and these great empires will only be permitted to continue for a limited time.

REFLECTION

There are many examples today of governments or individual rulers who wield great power, seem to have scant regard for God and at times appear to do as they please. Individual Christians (and others) often feel powerless, and the Church as a whole rarely seems to make any significant difference. How do we retain faith in God's sovereignty in such circumstances?

73

The PTOLEMIES & *the* SELEUCIDS

As noted previously, after the death of Alexander the Great, the Greek empire was divided into four parts. From verse 5 to verse 20, the focus is upon the conflict between the largest two of these parts: the Seleucid kingdom, which encompassed Syria, Babylonia and Persia, and the Ptolemaic kingdom of Egypt. These two kingdoms vied for control of Palestine, but it remained mostly under Ptolemaic control from about 322 to 198BC, after which control passed to the Seleucids under Antiochus III the Great. Antiochus IV Epiphanes was also a Seleucid ruler, and the last part of the chapter focuses on him and the impact he had on life in Palestine.

South and north

References to a 'king of the south' indicate a Ptolemaic king. The first such king (v. 5) was Ptolemy I Soter, who ruled from 323 to 282BC. He was one of Alexander's generals, among whom the Greek empire was divided. Initially he ruled as 'satrap' (governor of a province of the empire), but in 305BC he declared himself king and his dynasty was established. Seleucus I Nicator was satrap of Babylonia, but was ousted by Antigonus of Asia Minor in 316BC. He fled to Egypt and became a general in Ptolemy's army. Ptolemy and Seleucus defeated Antigonus in 312, and Seleucus regained control of Babylonia, set himself up as king and eventually established a kingdom which was much bigger than Ptolemy's kingdom. He is the first 'king of the north', a phrase that indicates a Seleucid king. Seleucus I ruled from 312 to 280BC, and was succeeded by Antiochus I Soter (280–261), who does not feature in Daniel. However, his successor, Antiochus II Theos (261–242) is 'the king of the north' in verse 6, who married 'the daughter of the king of the south'.

The king of the south in question is Ptolemy II Philadelphus (285–246), who made an alliance with Antiochus II by giving him his daughter Berenice in marriage, around 250BC. However, Antiochus II was already married to Laodice and had two sons, Seleucus and Antiochus. He left Laodice, and effectively disinherited his sons, to marry Berenice. She also bore him a son, but he returned to Laodice about two years later. It seems that Laodice murdered Antiochus II,

Berenice and their child, thus ensuring that her own son came to the throne as Seleucus II Callinicus (246–226), 'the king of the north' of verse 7. Berenice's father died the same year and was succeeded by her brother, Ptolemy III Euergetes (246–221), the 'branch from her roots' in verse 7.

Shifting power

Ptolemy III launched a campaign against the Seleucid kingdom, apparently because of the murder of his sister, and had a large measure of success (v. 8). He killed Laodice, captured Syria and made considerable inroads into the northern kingdom. He took much booty, and regained the gods that the Persians had removed from Egypt in 525BC. An uprising at home required him to return to Egypt, and Seleucus II re-established his kingdom and even tried to invade Egypt itself. He was unsuccessful, though, and had to retreat (v. 9). Seleucus II was succeeded by Seleucus III Soter Ceraunus (226–223), who in turn was succeeded by Antiochus III Magnus (223–187): these are the 'sons' described in verse 10. In the rest of verse 10, 'the multitude of great forces' and the 'advance like a flood' describe Antiochus III's considerable military success, which earned him the title 'the Great'. He pushed back down through Palestine and again threatened Egypt. He is 'the king of the north' mentioned throughout verses 11–19.

The next 'king of the south' (v. 11) was Ptolemy IV Philopator (221–203). He raised a large army and, in 217BC, engaged Antiochus III in battle. Antiochus III was badly defeated, losing very many of his men, but Ptolemy IV did not press home his advantage, and instead made peace with Antiochus. Antiochus then concentrated his efforts on expanding his territory in Asia Minor (Turkey) and further east, where he made significant gains. On the other hand, Ptolemy died in mysterious circumstances at the age of only about 35, along with his wife. He was succeeded by the six-year-old Ptolemy V Epiphanes (203–181).

REFLECTION

It is notable that God does not feature at all in this part of Daniel. Perhaps it is almost inevitable that when God is left out of the equation, individual or collective self-interest takes over and results in constant battling between different individuals or interest groups.

The ONE *who* ACTS *as* HE PLEASES

This passage focuses particularly on Antiochus III Magnus (223–187) in the north, and Ptolemy V Epiphanes (203–181) in the south. Seleucus IV Philopator is mentioned briefly in verse 20, which refers to his sending his prime minister, Heliodorus, in an unsuccessful attempt to pillage the Jerusalem temple. (It seems that Heliodorus may have been responsible for Seleucus IV's assassination in 175BC.)

The lawless among your own people

It is unclear just who the 'lawless' ones were (v. 14). It may be that they were pro-Seleucid Jews who supported Antiochus in his advance upon Jerusalem. It is not clear, though, why these people would be said to 'fail', as, despite a setback (when the Ptolemies recaptured Jerusalem under the general Scopas), Antiochus was successful in capturing Judah and Jerusalem, which then remained under Seleucid control. Alternatively, the 'lawless' ones may be a pro-Ptolemaic group who would have resisted the Seleucid advance, but certainly did fail in the end. In either case, it is also unclear what 'in order to fulfil the vision' refers to, although it might mean the vision in chapter 8. At any rate, these were collaborators with one or other Greek kingdom, who were perceived as transgressing the Jewish law.

Taking a position in the beautiful land

Antiochus III is described in verse 16 as taking 'a position in the beautiful land', after which 'all of it shall be in his power'. This refers to Antiochus' capture of Palestine in 198BC. This is the most significant element of the passage: after Palestine has remained mostly under the control of the Ptolemies (of Egypt) for most of the preceding 130 years, control now passes to the Seleucids (of Syria) under Antiochus III, never to return to the Ptolemies. Judah is referred to as 'the beautiful land' also in Daniel 8:9 and 11:41, and Zion is described as 'the beautiful holy mountain' in 11:45.

Give him a woman in marriage

Antiochus III sought to consolidate his power by offering his daughter Cleopatra in marriage to Ptolemy V (v. 17; see also 11:6, where

Ptolemy II gave his daughter Berenice in marriage to Antiochus II). Antiochus seems to have thought that Cleopatra would favour Seleucid interests and help him gain control over the Ptolemaic throne. Cleopatra was loyal to her husband, however, and even ruled as regent herself from the time of his death in 182BC until she died in 173BC.

An end to his insolence

A link is made between the 'warrior king' Alexander the Great, Antiochus III Magnus and Antiochus IV Epiphanes, because it is said of all three that they acted as they pleased (11:3, 16, 36). This is an important theme in the chapter: powerful kings appear to do whatever they want. Antiochus III's 'insolence' is also referred to twice in verse 18. He continued to expand his empire in Asia Minor and, despite warnings from Rome, tried to invade Greece in 192BC. Antiochus was soundly defeated by the Romans in 191BC, who thus 'turned his insolence back upon him'. The Romans imposed a humiliating treaty on Antiochus, and he was forced to retreat to his own lands (v. 19), where he was assassinated in 187BC during an attempt to pillage a temple so as to pay his tribute to Rome. Thus, it was his own pride in trying to expand his empire that eventually led to his downfall.

The arrogance of powerful rulers is a theme that we have noted before in Daniel, and it continues as a key aspect of chapter 11. Not only does the powerful king Antiochus III Magnus 'take the action he pleases', but he also involves others in his schemes. Some of the Jews collaborated with him (or possibly against him), with the result that they were unfaithful to their own laws. Antiochus even tried to use his own daughter as a pawn, but on that occasion the advantage went to his opponent. When power is abused (whether in international or national politics, or in community, church or family relationships), not only do other people get hurt, but people also get sucked in and often end up acting against their own consciences or religious beliefs.

PRAYER

Sovereign God, help the powerful rulers of our world to use their power well, and bring down those regimes where there is great abuse of power.

The CONTEMPTIBLE PERSON

With this section, we reach the central focus of the vision in chapters 10—12, concerning the Seleucid ruler Antiochus IV Epiphanes (175–164). Having raced through the Persian period in one verse, written off Alexander the Great in two verses, then alluded to five Ptolemaic kings and six Seleucid kings in 16 verses, the chapter now devotes 25 verses to Antiochus IV.

It is not absolutely clear how Antiochus IV came to rule. It is clear, though, that he was not the obvious successor to Seleucus IV, and that he gained the throne by dubious means: hence, he is described as 'a contemptible person on whom royal majesty had not been conferred' who obtained 'the kingdom through intrigue' in verse 21.

The word translated in verses 21 and 24 as 'without warning' literally means 'in quietness'. It is used in Daniel only of Antiochus (see also 8:25), and might be translated as 'by stealth'. It seems that Antiochus took the throne 'by stealth' and continued 'by stealth' to expand his influence, particularly in this case in Judah. The details of the intrigues surrounding these two dynasties are complex and rather bewildering (interested readers may wish to read Seow p. 176, where he tries to string together the available data). However, they illustrate the amazing complexities of power struggles the world over, including, of course, the current political situation in the Middle East, where the tract of land known as Israel or Palestine continues to be caught in the middle of bigger struggles.

The prince of the covenant

'The prince of the covenant' in verse 22 probably refers to the Jewish high priest Onias III, who was opposed to the imposition of Greek culture on the Jews. Under Antiochus III, the Jews were permitted self-governance according to the Torah, with the high priest effectively in charge. The high priestly office was a hereditary one, but in 175BC Antiochus IV, who sought to promulgate Greek practices wherever he went, made Onias' brother Jason high priest when Jason offered him a large bribe and assurances that he would institute a programme of hellenization in Jerusalem. In 172BC, Menelaus, who was from the powerful pro-Seleucid Tobiad family and therefore not even of the high priestly line, offered an even larger bribe, and was made high priest instead of Jason. The 'small party' referred to in verse 23 is probably Antiochus IV's Tobiad (and other) supporters—who may also be the 'richest people of the province' (v. 24: the word translated 'parts' in the NRSV could equally be 'people'), whom Antiochus rewarded lavishly for their support.

But only for a time

The words with which this section closes, 'but only for a time', are just two short words in Hebrew, but they are very important words. They introduce us to a key theme in the remaining verses of this chapter: a time is appointed (by God) for the end of the atrocities that Antiochus IV instigated. We met this theme in chapter 8, where Gabriel told Daniel that his vision was 'for the time of the end' (8:17) and explained that 'it refers to the appointed time of the end' (8:19).

Antiochus has been described as a 'wheeler-dealer', but this is a pretty mild term for so contemptible a person. We noted in the last section the arrogance of powerful rulers who appear to act as they please, and this arrogance comes to a climax with Antiochus IV. He epitomizes those who use whatever means they can to obtain the ends they want—even if that involves disposing of people who stand in their way and richly rewarding those who support them, acting with intrigue and deceit, and riding roughshod over other people's rights and beliefs. No wonder he was considered contemptible! There have been many other people in history and today who 'wheel and deal' in any way possible in order to achieve their own ends. Perhaps this tendency exists within most of us.

REFLECTION

How do we, and how should we, as Christians, respond when other people scheme their way to the top? How do we, and how should we, respond to such tendencies within ourselves?

TIMING IS EVERYTHING

This section introduces us to the final Ptolemaic king, Ptolemy VI Philometor (181–146), who is 'the king of the south' referred to in verse 25. Ptolemy VI of Egypt was also the nephew of Antiochus IV of Syria, as his mother Cleopatra, who acted as regent of Egypt following the death of Ptolemy V, was Antiochus' sister. The power struggles recorded in these verses really are a family affair!

The Memphis 'summit'

Ptolemy VI set out in 170BC to recapture Palestine, so Antiochus IV went into battle against him. Antiochus soundly defeated the Egyptians, occupied significant swathes of Egypt, and then took Ptolemy VI himself captive. It seems that courtiers who had advised Ptolemy VI to attack Palestine then set up his younger brother, Ptolemy VII, as king. This may be what is referred to in verses 25–26: 'But he shall not succeed, for plots shall be devised against him by those who eat of the royal rations.' Antiochus descended on Memphis, where he formed a pact with the defeated Ptolemy VI and helped him to recover the throne—no doubt because he hoped to have a puppet king on the Egyptian throne. It is probably this Memphis 'summit' (Seow's word, p. 179) that is alluded to in verse 27: 'The two kings, their minds bent on evil, shall sit at one table and exchange lies.' This highlights the fact that both kings had their own agendas and were playing for any advantage they could get. However, the two Ptolemy brothers formed an alliance (apparently at the instigation of their sister Cleopatra, of the same name as her mother—but note that the Cleopatra in Shakespeare's *Antony and Cleopatra* comes much later) and became joint rulers of Egypt. Antiochus was then unable to make further inroads into the country. He did try to invade Egypt again in 168BC, but this time he was turned away in humiliating fashion by the Romans (indicated by the 'ships of Kittim' in 11:30). These verses thus make clear that the intrigue and family wheeling and dealing continued. Different members of the same family were playing power games at the cost of many, many innocent lives.

At the time appointed

References to 'time' punctuate the final verses of the book of Daniel. We noted in the last section that Antiochus' atrocities would be 'only for a time' (11:24). Verse 27 then states that 'there remains an end at the time appointed'. This is picked up in 11:29 with the words, 'At the time appointed'; 11:35 concludes, '... until the time of the end, for there is still an interval until the time appointed'; 11:40 starts, 'At the time of the end'. Then 12:1 has three references to time (actually four in Hebrew): 'at that time', 'there shall be a time' and 'at that time' again. Verse 4 of chapter 12 refers once more to 'the time of the end'. The phrase 'time, two times, and half a time' appears again in 12:7, and 'the time of the end' is used again in 12:9. As we noted above, 12:11 starts with the words, 'From the time that the regular burnt-offering is taken away and the abomination that desolates is set up...' Thus, twelve time references appear in these two final chapters. This emphasizes the extent to which it is a key theme in the concluding part of the book of Daniel. It demonstrates that, dreadful as things may have seemed under Antiochus IV Epiphanes, and much as he played his endless power games, his times were in the hands of the God who ultimately controls the times at which events unfold. As we have noted before, Antiochus' days were, quite literally, numbered.

This heavy emphasis on the appointed times is typical of apocalyptic literature. There is a danger that this might be seen as deterministic, suggesting that we have no freedom because God determines ahead of time what will happen. This does not appear to be the case here, though: rather, God allows people considerable freedom in how they act. Antiochus IV Epiphanes clearly used, or rather abused, this freedom to the full—but God ultimately sets limits and establishes the 'times' when evil will be brought to an end and good will triumph.

REFLECTION

Psalm 31:15 states, 'My times are in your hands.' How do you understand this in relation to your own life? To what extent does it seem that God allows you freedom to act as you will, and to what extent does he 'determine the times'?

The HOLY COVENANT

The rest of chapter 11 narrows its focus, to home in on Antiochus IV Epiphanes and his impact on Judah and Jerusalem. This means that the final vision in the book of Daniel builds up to a focus on Antiochus IV, as was the case in earlier chapters as well. Thus I, along with most scholars today (but not all), believe that Antiochus IV is represented by 'the little horn' which is a key aspect of the vision in chapter 7. 'The little horn' in chapter 8 was the climax of the vision in that chapter, and almost all commentators agree that this refers to Antiochus IV. I also think, as again many others do (but not all), that the end of chapter 9 alludes to events associated with Antiochus IV's reign and that he is the 'desolator' whose end the final verse of that chapter anticipates. This would mean that Antiochus IV features in the vision in chapter 7, and that the final three visions of the book (in chapters 8—12, which are the Hebrew chapters as opposed to the Aramaic chapters 2—7) all build up to Antiochus IV and events associated with his reign. The marked difference in the final vision is that it moves, in chapter 12, beyond Antiochus' death to consider what will happen afterwards. This considerable emphasis on Antiochus seems to be strong evidence for dating the last five chapters to the second century BC, when the Jews were actually suffering under his rule.

The covenant

'The holy covenant' features only here in Daniel (and indeed nowhere else in the Old Testament), and it is repeated three times in these verses. The phrase seems to denote the covenant people, and is thus similar to the 'people of the holy ones' in 7:27 and the 'holy people' in 12:7. We might recall that Antiochus deposed the legitimate high priest, Onias III, who was described in 11:22 as 'the prince of the covenant'; and 'those who forsake the holy covenant' in verse 30 may be the same as 'those who violate the covenant' in 11:32. It seems that the high priest whom Antiochus set up in place of Onias III, Jason, who was himself then replaced by Menelaus, heard rumours that Antiochus had been killed in battle in Egypt, so he attacked Jerusalem and sought to regain control of it. Antiochus responded by sending troops to Jerusalem, where he slaughtered many of the Jews, re-established the Tobiad family (probably 'those who forsake the holy covenant' in v. 30) in control, tore down the walls of Jerusalem and instead built a garrison in the temple precincts. In addition, Antiochus issued an edict banning traditional Jewish religious practices: reading of the law was prohibited, the temple offerings were suspended, circumcision was banned, and altars to Greek gods were set up. Thus Antiochus' actions represent the antithesis of 'the holy covenant'.

The abomination that makes desolate

The final great insult that Antiochus issued to the Jews, and to their God, came when he set up an altar to the god Zeus in the Jerusalem temple and offered pigs on it. The fact that this is referred to a number of times in Daniel indicates that it was a cause of very great concern. It is mentioned first as 'the transgression that makes desolate' in 8:13. Then the phrase the 'abomination that desolates' occurs in 9:27, 11:31 and 12:11. In 12:11, 'the time that the regular burnt-offering is taken away and the abomination that desolates is set up' is the point from which time is measured until 'the time of the end'. All this does rather suggest that the event represented by the 'abomination that desolates' was a recent occurrence in the memory of the first Jewish readers of the book of Daniel, or at least of the Hebrew chapters, 8—12.

You will have gathered by now that there is much in these verses that repeats what we have found in earlier chapters. There is more detail here, however, and the emphases are different (although the repetition itself gives emphasis to the significance of the events associated with Antiochus IV). The Jews are characterized in this passage by 'holiness' and by the 'covenant': they were to be a holy people in covenant relationship with God. Although we are under a new covenant, the same is true for Christians today.

REFLECTION

What do you think it means for us to be a 'holy covenant' people?
What might be the equivalent today of the 'abomination'?

REMAINING LOYAL *to* GOD

This passage probably gives us some clues about who the author of this part of Daniel was, and what his circumstances were. It is likely that he was one of 'the wise', who saw themselves as 'loyal to their God', but also considered themselves in danger of falling 'by sword and flame' and suffering 'captivity and plunder'. 'Falling' is emphasized (it is repeated three times), and it rather looks as though this group did not anticipate receiving much support from elsewhere ('they shall receive a little help', v. 34). In other words, this author is one of a small, religious, 'faithful' group who are enduring persecution at the hands of Antiochus IV Epiphanes.

Seduced with intrigue

A contrast is drawn in verse 32 between those who are 'seduce[d] with intrigue' and 'violate the covenant' and those who 'are loyal to their God' and 'shall stand firm and take action'. Probably, the former are collaborators whom Antiochus rewarded richly (in other words, bribed) for their support. The latter are probably the group from which this vision derived—faithful Jews who stood up to the regime. It is possible that 'taking action' implies some endorsement of the Maccabean revolt, but this is rather out of keeping with the non-violent resistance propounded elsewhere in Daniel. More probably, then, it indicates those who refused to conform to Antiochus' restriction on Jewish worship, rather than those who took up arms in opposition to him. The word 'intrigue' is used only in verses relating to Antiochus. In 11:21 we read that he obtained 'the kingdom through intrigue'; here in verse 32 he 'seduce[s] with intrigue'; in verse 34 the same word is used in 'many shall join them *insincerely*'; and likewise in 11:39, 'he shall... *distribute* the land for a price'. The word derives from a root meaning 'smooth': Antiochus was a 'smooth operator' who won over many people by whatever means he could.

A third group is those who 'shall join them insincerely' (v. 34). These are probably people who say that they support the faithful group, but do nothing to display their support. Such people are likely to slip away when the heat gets turned up.

The wise among the people

There has been much discussion about just who the 'wise' were. They were probably well-educated Jews working in positions of some authority in the community, ultimately under the control of the occupying power. Their familiarity with the ways of this pagan culture, in addition to their study of their own sacred literature, would have enabled them to comment on current and past events in ways that would be understood by their intended readers but wouldn't necessarily be perceived as direct resistance to the pagan rulers. They were, it seems, attempting to remain faithful to God while also functioning effectively under an alien and oppressive regime (see Lucas, pp. 288–9, for more details).

A number of commentators argue, on the grounds of shared vocabulary, that the 'suffering servant' in Isaiah 52:13—53:12 lies in the background of this passage. This is possible, and would imply that the 'wise' acted, and perhaps suffered, on behalf of 'the many'—the faithful Jews. Such martyrdom is probably what lies behind the first half of verse 35: 'Some of the wise shall fall, so that they may be refined, purified, and cleansed.'

A little help

Scholars disagree over the precise implications of the phrase 'they shall receive a little help' (v. 34). Most see it as a sideswipe at the military resistance put up by the Maccabees (see, for example, Lederach, p. 246): according to Daniel, this is not the way in which God's victory will be achieved. Rather, it will be won through non-violent resistance, as exemplified in the first half of the book. I think that this is the most likely interpretation, although others see it as an acknowledgment that the Maccabean resistance was at least of some help (see Goldingay, p. 303). Still others explain it as a general comment on how little help the small faithful group received from anybody else (see Seow, p. 181).

REFLECTION

Can you think of examples from your own experience where some Christians have been 'seduced' into acting unfaithfully, where others have stood firm regardless of the consequence, and still others have said they remained faithful but their actions gave grounds for doubt about the sincerity of their words?

GREATER *than* ALL?

In these verses we find what looks like a summary of the offences that Antiochus committed, focusing primarily on his religious attitude. This emphasizes the challenge he issued not just to the Jews, but also to their God—and even to the gods of his own people.

Greater than any god

Words for 'god' appear more often in these four verses than anywhere else in Daniel: three times in verse 36, twice in verse 37, twice in verse 38, and once in verse 39. The first verse opens with words we have met before, 'The king shall act as he pleases', but the context here indicates that he does what he likes not only in relation to other people and other nations, but also in relation to the gods. This is indicated by the verbs used—'exalt himself' and 'consider himself great'—which else-where are applied to God or to those who challenge God. It may be picking up on the fact that Antiochus had the words 'of King Antiochus, God Manifest, Victory-Bringer' ('Victory-bringer' being an epithet used of the god Zeus) inscribed on his coins.

The word used for 'god' in verse 36 is a general word (*el*), which is applied to the Lord and also to other gods. However, the expression 'God of gods' (v. 36) in this context clearly relates to the Lord: Antiochus set himself up over even the Lord, the God of the Jews. His speaking 'horrendous things' recalls his arrogance in 7:8, 20, 25 and 8:11, but there is great irony in the expression used here: 'horrendous things' (which is used also of Antiochus' deeds in 8:24) might be ren-dered more neutrally as 'extraordinary things', and is used elsewhere to describe God's wonderful deeds (see Psalm 119:27).

Antiochus even sets himself up over the gods of his own people. A different word for 'god' is used in the remaining verses, which may in this context mean 'other god', a god other than the Lord. 'He shall pay no respect to the gods of his ancestors' (v. 37) probably indicates his preference for Zeus over Apollo, the god worshipped by the Seleucids. 'The one beloved of women', then, may indicate Adonis or Dionysius, popular gods in Egypt. This implies that Antiochus rejected the gods of both the Seleucids and the Ptolemies; he honoured instead 'the god of fortresses' (v. 38).

The god of fortresses

There has been much debate about what 'the god of fortresses' represents. It seems likely to me that it is the god worshipped by Antiochus' soldiers in the various fortresses he established in Judah, and particularly in Jerusalem. Seow is probably correct in his argument that, rather than being the Greek god Zeus Olympius, this was a warrior god who could readily be associated with the variety of different deities worshipped by the Syrian troops, and was even identified with the Lord by some Greek Jews. Hence, Antiochus could rally his troops around a 'common' god, and this suited his purposes well. Seow's conclusion is that 'apparently, religion was to Antiochus nothing but a tool, a convenient means to an end' (p. 183). It is one thing to be a follower of a religion other than Christianity, or even to be a sincere unbeliever, but it is quite another thing to use Christianity or any other religion for one's own selfish ends. This is patent in the case of Antiochus, who appeared to ride roughshod over the God of the Jews and even the gods of his own peoples. For many of us (most, or even all?), however, there is the tendency to use religion for our own purposes, at least to some extent.

What is determined shall be done

In the NRSV, the final phrase of verse 36 sounds decidedly deterministic, as though God has everything planned out beforehand. As indicated before, I don't think that this is what it means in the context. It seems clear that God allowed the Persian and Greek rulers considerable freedom, but did establish limits: the God portrayed in Daniel has ultimate sovereignty and controls the 'times' of these rulers, ensuring an 'end' to their wickedness. It should be said, though, that apocalyptic literature does tend towards determinism, and as the author of Daniel 7—12 draws on this genre, there may also be a tendency in this direction here.

PRAYER

Sovereign God, thwart the purposes of those who patently use religion as a 'convenient means to an end', but also help us all to be aware of this tendency within ourselves and to overcome the tendency.

YET HE SHALL COME *to* HIS END

In a sense, this is the most difficult passage in the book. Up to this point, the events relating to the Persian and Greek rulers can mostly be confirmed from other sources as historically accurate. Many see in this the accuracy of Daniel's prophecy in the sixth century BC, up to 350 years or so before the events took place. Others see the 'prophecy' as a retelling of that history from a second-century perspective. In this section, however, the events related do not accord well with what we know about the end of Antiochus' life. Two diametrically opposed explanations of this are common. First, those who see the chapter as genuine prediction from the sixth century usually see a marked change occurring with the words in verse 40, 'At the time of the end', and read this section as relating to the distant future, well beyond Antiochus' time. Second, those who read the earlier parts of the chapter as 'prophecy after the event' perceive a change here to 'genuine prophecy' that simply proved to be wrong (see comments on p. 154). I will indicate an alternative approach in the next section.

According to Daniel

The various sources tell slightly different versions of Antiochus' final days, but they all agree that he undertook a campaign in Persia, during which he tried unsuccessfully to rob a temple (probably to raise much-needed funds). At about this time, in or just before December 164BC, he died, possibly because of a sudden illness. This course of events appears to bear no resemblance to Daniel 11:40–45.

If these final verses of chapter 11 are about Antiochus, as I believe they are, this is the picture they present. Ptolemy VI Philometor launched an attack on Antiochus' Syrian empire, to which Antiochus responded with great speed and considerable force (v. 40). He swept into Judah and other countries on his way to Egypt, killing many people but sparing some neighbouring countries, like Edom and Moab (v. 41). Next he turned his attention to Egypt itself, where he achieved considerable success and took much booty (vv. 42–43). He then moved on to other African countries, Libya and Ethiopia (v. 43). However, he heard bad news from his own empire (rumours of an insurrection, perhaps), and returned north, leaving devastation in his trail (v. 44). When he got to Judah, he established camp between the Mediterranean Sea and Jerusalem, but died there—although there is no indication of just how this happened (v. 45).

Is this about Antiochus?

The fact that Daniel's account of Antiochus' 'end' differs so greatly from the accounts in other sources raises the obvious question of whether these verses are about Antiochus at all. There is no clear indication that the passage should be read as anything other than a continuation of what went before, and the 'him' of verse 40 most obviously picks up on Antiochus in the previous section. We have seen references to 'time' and to 'the end' occurring repeatedly throughout the chapter, and particularly in the second half, once the focus shifts on to Antiochus. In that context, 'the time of the end' here (and in 8:19; 11:27, 35) seems to refer to the end of the persecution that the Jews were suffering at Antiochus' hand, rather than an eschatological 'end'.

It makes sense for the chapter to conclude by portraying Antiochus' 'end' as it was promised earlier in the chapter. Moreover, the 'end' is described using key themes and words from earlier verses. A key aspect of the chapter has been the constant battles between 'kings of the north' and 'kings of the south', which come to a head in these final verses of the chapter. The impact that these battles have had on Judah and Jerusalem has become an increasingly significant element in the chapter; in this section, Antiochus comes for the last time to Judah, and finally dies just outside Jerusalem (indicated by 'the beautiful holy mountain', Zion, upon which Jerusalem was built, v. 45). Even if this is not historically accurate, it is important symbolically.

People often discover discrepancies between what they read in scripture and how they perceive things to be 'in reality'. This seems to be the case in the final verses of Daniel 11, but it occurs elsewhere in the Old Testament, and in the New Testament. Both, in my experience, are fairly regular parts of day-to-day Christian living, and I think they need not cause concern.

REFLECTION

Does this correlate with your experience or that of other people you know. If so, how do you handle such 'discrepancies'?

ANTIOCHUS & BIBLICAL PROPHECY

Having raised, in the last section, the issue of the apparent discrepancy between the description of Antiochus' 'end' in verses 40–45 and what we know from elsewhere of his final days, in this section I will suggest a possible explanation. First, though, it would be helpful to consider the ways in which this passage draws on other Old Testament prophetic texts.

In the light of the prophets

Lederach states that the writer of Daniel 11 'clothes the demise of Antiochus not in a veiled recounting of history but with scriptural allusions to show that as God acted in the past, so he would soon act to alleviate the present crisis' (p. 251). Thus, it seems that Antiochus is portrayed as 'the foe from the north', a typical description of the nations that threaten Judah in Jeremiah (see, for example, Jeremiah 1:14 and 50:3, where the word 'desolation' occurs). The attacks of the Seleucid forces are also portrayed using language from Isaiah's prophecies about Assyria. Thus, for example, the expression in verse 40, 'pass through like a flood', probably picks up the description of Assyria in Isaiah 8:8: 'it will sweep on into Judah as a flood'.

The 'rumours' that caused Antiochus to return towards Syria may draw on what is said about the Assyrian ruler Sennacherib in Isaiah 37:7: 'I myself will put a spirit in him, so that he shall hear a rumour, and return to his own land.' Antiochus' return to Judah 'with great fury', setting up 'his palatial tents between the sea and the beautiful mountain', may draw on the Assyrians in Isaiah 10:32, of whom it is said, 'he will shake his fist at the mount of daughter Zion, the hill of Jerusalem'. It may be that Antiochus' final demise near Jerusalem builds on such passages as Joel 3:2, 'I will gather all the nations and bring them down to the valley of Jehoshaphat' (see also Ezekiel 39:2–4). In these and other ways, the writer of Daniel 11 makes extensive use of earlier biblical prophecy in his portrayal of Antiochus' final days. In earlier prophecies, a foe like the Assyrians or the Babylonians had swept down upon Israel or Judah from the north, but, in spite of their apparent success, God had eventually brought about their end as he had promised he would. The same will happen, Daniel assures us, in relation to Antiochus IV Epiphanes.

A possible explanation

If this chapter derives from around 165BC (in other words, after the setting up of 'the abomination that desolates' but before Antiochus' death), it may be that the writer has portrayed the past 350 years of Judah's subjection to foreign powers as an apocalyptic vision of the sixth-century Daniel, alluding to various Old Testament prophets on the way. This portrayal has shown that, despite the scheming and intrigues of the various kings, ultimately the Lord, the God of the Jews, was in control of their 'times'. The vision comes to its climax with contemporary events: persecution at the hand of Antiochus IV Epiphanes. Developing from the portrayal of past history, the writer proceeds to paint an imaginative picture of the imminent future, again using the apocalyptic genre and other Old Testament prophets as his medium for that portrayal. Thus, rather than being a detailed prediction of what will happen to Antiochus, it is a picture of the kind of thing that must happen to him in light of past history and his recent defiance of God. As such, it certainly did come true! A reading roughly along these lines is adopted by a number of recent commentators (see, for example, Goldingay, Lederach, Lucas, Redditt, Seow).

Biblical prophecy is not primarily about prediction and fulfilment. Rather, it is 'the interpretation of the will of God in the socio-political and historical arena' (Seow, p. 185), which does include some element of prediction. The prophets appear to have been people who had great insight into the political, social and religious issues of their day, as well as a deep understanding of their own religious traditions and the will of God.

In line with this, I would maintain that the value of Daniel 11 lies not in the accuracy of its supposed 'predictions' but in the insight it offers, drawing extensively on earlier biblical texts, into how God was and is engaged with the earthly (and, in chapter 10, the heavenly) powers that, to a greater or lesser extent, control our lives.

REFLECTION

What implications does this reading have for our understanding of biblical prophecy, and of prophecy today?

RESURRECTION

The focus on Antiochus IV Epiphanes, to which the whole of chapter 11 was building up, is finished. Now the focus shifts back to the heavenly realm and picks up where chapter 10 left off, with the patron angel Michael. It would be a mistake to think that chapter 12 suddenly jumps to some great eschatological event in the distant future: it continues where chapter 11 finished, but, while the vision in chapter 11 provided an overview of the earthly scene, chapter 12 now gives insight into the heavenly side of the equation, which helps to bring a very different perspective on the events of the second century BC and beyond.

At that time

'At that time' in verse 1 picks up on earlier references to time, especially 11:40, which starts with exactly the same word ('and-at-time', one word in Hebrew). In turn, 11:40 picks up on the expression 'only for a time' in 11:24, and 'until the time of the end' in 11:35. 'Until the time of the end' then occurs again in 12:4 and 9. A different word for 'time', with the sense of 'appointed time', occurs in 11:27, 29, 35 and 12:7. We should recall that the word for 'time' is used four times in 12:1. This indicates two things: firstly, the continuing importance of the theme of 'time' in chapter 12, and secondly, that 'that time' in verse 1 is the same time referred to earlier, which I have argued is the time of Antiochus IV's 'end'. This means that, although Antiochus is not mentioned again, the events alluded to here are still associated with him: the 'time of anguish' refers to the suffering under Antiochus, and 'the time of the end' in verse 4 is the time when this anguish ceases (presumably upon Antiochus' death).

The book

'The book' is mentioned twice in this passage (vv. 1, 4), but it is probably a different book from the others referred to in Daniel. 'Books' of judgment feature in 7:10. In 9:2 Daniel refers to the 'books' that contain the words of Jeremiah. Then, 10:21 mentions 'the book of truth', but a different Hebrew word is used, which might be translated as 'the writings'. The book here in chapter 12 seems to be a roll of 'membership of the covenantal community' (Collins, p. 391), a concept found elsewhere in the Old Testament (Exodus 32:32–33; Psalm 69:28; Isaiah 4:3; Malachi 3:16–18). Such a 'book of life' features often in Revelation (3:5; 13:8; 17:8; 20:12, 15; 21:27). The 'sealing' of the book probably ties in with the ascription of the vision to the sixth-century Daniel. The secrets of the book are to be guarded until such time as they will make sense to the readers —that is, those suffering under Antiochus IV Epiphanes. This is typical of the pseudepigraphal literature of the time (that is, later works attributed to an ancient worthy, like the second-century *Book of Enoch*).

Resurrection

Verse 2 is the only unambiguous reference to resurrection in the Old Testament. Moreover, it is a double resurrection, because some are raised to everlasting life while others are raised to 'shame and everlasting contempt'. This is very significant in the development of the idea of resurrection, which, soon after the time of Daniel, became an important concept in some parts of Judaism and, of course, is a key element in Christian doctrine. The developed Christian doctrine of resurrection should not be read into these verses, however: it must be borne in mind that the immediate context is the second century BC and the end of Antiochus' persecutions. Moreover, it is 'many' and not all that are raised, and the 'many' here probably refers to Jews, as it does elsewhere in Daniel (see 11:33, 39, 44; 12:3). The faithful Jews will be raised to everlasting life, and the faithless Jews to judgment.

The wise

The 'wise' come in for special mention here again and, in these verses, form a particularly stark contrast with Antiochus. The description of the wise as 'those who lead many to righteousness' may well pick up again on the 'suffering servant' in Isaiah 52:13—53:12: 'The righteous one, my servant, shall make many righteous' (53:11).

PRAYER

Sovereign God, may the hope of resurrection be a source of great comfort to those who are 'found written in the book', especially those for whom life now is extremely difficult.

HAPPY ARE THOSE *who* PERSEVERE

This section constitutes an epilogue to the vision and to the book as a whole. It picks up on the introduction to the vision in 10:1—11:1 and, with that earlier passage, forms a frame around the vision. These verses introduce nothing that is really new, but rather draw together a number of threads from chapters 10—12, and, indeed, even earlier in Daniel, to form a summarizing conclusion to the book.

How long?

'How long?' is the key question addressed in these verses, and in this they pick up on a similar passage in 8:13–14, where the answer is given: 'For two thousand three hundred evenings and mornings; then the sanctuary shall be restored to its rightful state.' Of course, the 'time, two times and half a time' recurs here (v. 7), using the word for 'appointed time' that occurs in 11:27, 29, 35 (and 8:19). It is certainly possible that the week and the 2300 evenings and mornings both indicate a period of about seven years, and that half a week and 'a time, two times and half a time' represent the approximately three and a half years during which the offerings were prohibited at the sanctuary. (2300 evenings and mornings might indicate this shorter period if an evening plus a morning is one day.) In that case, 1290 days (v. 11) may be a more accurate figure for this same period, and 1335 days (v. 12) would then be either a correction in light of what actually happened or a reference to a slightly later event. So the first figure could be the period until the sacrifice was re-established and the second until Antiochus' death, or perhaps vice versa. This is possible, but we can't know for certain, and it seems foolish to worry about it when the scholars can't agree about the precise references here. The point is surely one that we have noted a number of times already: the 'times' are in God's hands and Antiochus' days are numbered. Thus, there is hope beyond the dreadful circumstances of the present.

In summary

This passage picks up on the introduction to the vision in chapter 10, and has links back to earlier chapters. Thus it reiterates the 'time, two times and half a time' from 7:25, emphasizing again the importance of the restricted period of Antiochus' persecution. Reference to 'the holy people' (v. 7) picks up on 'the holy ones' and 'the people of the holy ones' in 7:18, 21, 25, 27, but specifies here that it is holy people who are in view. 'All these things' that will 'be accomplished' (v. 7) refers back to the end of chapter 11 and the beginning of chapter 12, the demise of Antiochus and the corresponding blessings for the Jews. These blessings include being 'purified, cleansed and refined' (v. 10), which is picked up from 11:35 but extended this time beyond the 'wise' to 'the many'—that is, the faithful Jews. Keeping the words 'secret and sealed until the time of the end' is repeated almost word for word from 12:4. Daniel's inability to understand is a theme we have met often in earlier chapters, but here such lack of understanding is resolved: at the time of the end, the wise shall understand (v. 10). Finally, 'the abomination that desolates' features again (v. 11).

Repetition is used here to reiterate key themes from the visions in the second half of the book of Daniel. God controls the times; an end to the suffering of the faithful Jews is in sight; all the things described earlier in chapters 11 and 12 will come to pass, including the Jews being purified, cleansed and refined. Until they happen, people will not understand them, so they need to be kept secret; but when they do come to pass, the wise will understand. Finally, the abomination that desolates is a key focus of the persecutions that the Jews have been suffering.

And in conclusion …

The conclusion is clear: 'happy are those who persevere' (v. 12), and presumably they, like Daniel, will rise for their reward at the end of the days. Times may be dreadful, but if people remain faithful and persevere, they will be blessed (another translation for the word 'happy') and will rise to receive their reward in the end. The 'end' is reiterated in the Hebrew of verse 13 (this isn't obvious in English), and although it probably still refers to the end of Antiochus' persecution, it has relevance beyond that. It is possible, of course, for faithful people, now as then, to suffer until their death, but the message of Daniel is that if they persevere they will know blessing and receive their reward in the end.

PRAYER

Lord God, help us to persevere and to have a solid hope in you
as a God who ultimately is sovereign and will ensure that
justice is done in the end.

NOTES

NOTES

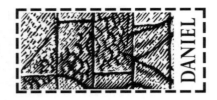

DANIEL

THE PEOPLE'S
BIBLE COMMENTARY

VOUCHER SCHEME

The People's Bible Commentary (PBC) provides a range of readable, accessible commentaries that will grow into a library covering the whole Bible.

To help you build your PBC library, we have a voucher scheme that works as follows: a voucher is printed on this page of each People's Bible Commentary volume (as above). These vouchers count towards free copies of other books in the series.

For every four purchases of PBC volumes you are entitled to a further volume FREE.

Please find the coupon for the PBC voucher scheme opposite.

All you need do:

- Cut out the vouchers from the PBCs you have purchased and attach them to the coupon.

- Complete your name and address details, and indicate your choice of free book from the list on page 192.

- Take the coupon to your local Christian bookshop who will exchange it for your free PBC book; or send the coupon straight to BRF who will send you your free book direct. Please allow 28 days for delivery.

Please note that PBC volumes provided under the voucher scheme are subject to availability. If your first choice is not available, you may be sent your second choice of book.

THE PEOPLE'S
BIBLE COMMENTARY

VOUCHER SCHEME COUPON

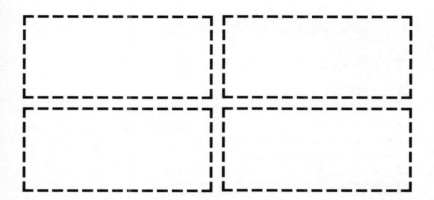

Customer and bookseller should both complete the form overleaf.

Name: ....

Address: ....

. . . .

Postcode: ....

My choice of free PBC volume is:
(Please indicate a first and second choice;
all volumes are supplied subject to
availability.)

☐ Genesis
☐ Exodus
☐ Leviticus and Numbers
☐ Deuteronomy
☐ Joshua and Judges
☐ Ruth, Esther, Ecclesiastes,
   Song of Songs, Lamentations
☐ 1 & 2 Samuel
☐ 1 & 2 Kings
☐ Chronicles to Nehemiah
☐ Job
☐ Psalms 1—72
☐ Psalms 73—150
☐ Proverbs
☐ Isaiah
☐ Jeremiah
☐ Ezekiel
☐ Daniel
☐ Hosea to Micah
☐ Nahum to Malachi
☐ Matthew
☐ Mark
☐ Luke
☐ John
☐ Acts
☐ Romans
☐ 1 Corinthians
☐ 2 Corinthians
☐ Galatians and Thessalonians

☐ Ephesians to Colossians
   and Philemon
☐ Timothy, Titus and Hebrews
☐ James to Jude
☐ Revelation

TO BE COMPLETED BY THE BOOKSELLER

(Please complete the following.
Coupons redeemed will be credited to
your account for the value of the
book(s) supplied as indicated above.
Please note that only coupons correctly
completed with original vouchers will
be accepted for credit.)

Name: ....

Address: ....

. . . .

Postcode: ....

Account Number: ....

Completed coupons should be
sent to: BRF, PBC Voucher
Scheme, First Floor, Elsfield Hall,
15–17 Elsfield Way, Oxford
OX2 8FG.

Tel 01865 319700; Fax 01865
319701; e-mail enquiries@brf.org.uk
Registered Charity No. 233280

**THIS OFFER IS AVAILABLE IN THE UK
ONLY**
**PLEASE NOTE: ALL VOUCHERS ATTACHED
TO THE COUPON MUST BE ORIGINAL
COPIES.**